# Contents

# Author Preface and Acknowledgements

This text has been written specifically to assist teachers and students to meet the requirements of CCEA's Government and Politics AS Unit 1, 'The Government and Politics of Northern Ireland'. Within the introduction, the book will look at the historical background leading up to 1998, (although this will not be the specific focus of examination questions), and the remaining four sections match the topics listed in the relevant section of CCEA's specification: The Northern Ireland Assembly (which has been divided into two distinct sections, The Four Agreements and The Northern Ireland Assembly); The Executive Committee; and The Northern Ireland Political Parties.

I would like to express my appreciation to my close colleagues and dear friends, Dennis Norman and John Martin, whose support in my early and developing career was an invaluable base for this project. I also wish to acknowledge the help provided by my editor, Michelle Griffin, whose suggestions were always cogent and the execution of which have undoubtedly made this book better. Finally I want to thank my family whose unerring patience and support is the bedrock upon which all of my achievements rest. A special thanks should go to my husband Paul who is a constant encouragement, and without whom I may well have given up several times along the way.

Lesley Veronica
November 2017

# Abbreviations

| | |
|---|---|
| **AIA** | Anglo-Irish Agreement |
| **APNI** | Alliance Party NI |
| **CLMC** | Combined Loyalist Military Command |
| **CRM** | Civil Rights Movement |
| **CVSNI** | Commission for Victims and Survivors NI |
| **DETI** | Department of Enterprise, Trade and Investment |
| **DSD** | Department for Social Development |
| **DUP** | Democratic Unionist Party |
| **ECHR** | European Convention on Human Rights |
| **EEC** | European Economic Community (now EU) |
| **EU** | European Union |
| **FARC** | Revolutionary Armed Forces of Columbia |
| **GAA** | Gaelic Athletic Association |
| **GFA** | Good Friday Agreement |
| **HCA** | Hillsborough Castle Agreement |
| **HET** | Historical Enquiries Team |
| **IGC** | Intergovernmental Conference |
| **INLA** | Irish National Liberation Army |
| **IRA** | Irish Republican Army |
| **LVF** | Loyalist Volunteer Force |
| **MLA** | Member of the Legislative Assembly |
| **NI** | Northern Ireland |
| **NICRA** | Northern Ireland Civil Rights Association |
| **NIO** | Northern Ireland Office |
| **NMSC** | North South Ministerial Council |
| **OFMdFM** | Office of the First Minister and deputy First Minister (now the Executive Office) |
| **PfG** | Programme for Government |
| **PIRA** | Provisional IRA |

| | |
|---|---|
| **PSNI** | Police Service of Northern Ireland |
| **PUP** | Progressive Unionist Party |
| **RHC** | Red Hand Commando |
| **RHI** | Renewable Heat Incentive |
| **RoI** | Republic of Ireland |
| **RUC** | Royal Ulster Constabulary |
| **SDLP** | Social Democratic and Labour Party |
| **SHA** | Stormont House Agreement |
| **STV** | single transferable vote |
| **TUV** | Traditional Unionist Voice |
| **UCUNF** | Ulster Conservatives and Unionists: New Force |
| **UDA** | Ulster Defence association |
| **UDR** | Ulster Defence Regiment |
| **UFF** | Ulster Freedom Fighters |
| **UKIP** | United Kingdom Independence Party |
| **UKUP** | United Kingdom Unionist Party |
| **UUP** | Ulster Unionist Party |
| **UVF** | Ulster Volunteer Force |
| **UWC** | Ulster Workers' Council |
| **WCNI** | Womens' Coalition NI |

# Introduction

In 1998, the Belfast Agreement – more commonly referred to as the Good Friday Agreement (GFA)[1] – established the political institutions for Northern Ireland (NI). Since then there have been many changes in both the operation of the institutions and in the priorities of the political parties. There have been three subsequent agreements to update the arrangements originally laid down by the Good Friday Agreement – St Andrews, Hillsborough and Stormont House – all of which have extended or clarified certain aspects of the original agreement in an attempt to make the political institutions more workable. Students need to have a brief but clear knowledge of these subsequent agreements and how they have impacted devolution.

Currently Sinn Féin and the Democratic Unionist Party (DUP) are the dominant political parties, with both the Ulster Unionist Party (UUP) and the Social Democratic Labour Party (SDLP) struggling to regain their previously dominant positions, and new political parties, and issues are coming to the fore. Other changes, such as the reduction of government departments in the Executive and the setting up of an opposition, also need to be accounted for. Given the changing political environment and procedural changes in the operation of devolution a new book outlining the current arrangements seemed timely and necessary for students to be able to tackle the subject area with confidence.

This book is designed to build upon the firm foundation set by Margery McMahon's *Government and Politics of Northern Ireland* (2002; revised 2008), aimed at NI A level Politics students to address NI-specific political institutions. Rapid changes since 2008 have necessitated a more current account to help students and teachers preparing for the CCEA Government and Politics AS Unit 1, 'The Government and Politics of Northern Ireland'. The significant changes brought about by the St Andrew's Agreement in 2008 resulted in the first full Assembly and Executive, so knowledge of the period following 2008 is essential if students are to analyse the performance of the institutions. This post-2008 focus is likewise reflected in the specification, and although there is a need for some knowledge of the period before 2008, this is at a minimum. This book aims, therefore, to provide students with an account that is as up-to-date as possible and which best meets the needs of the current specification. It has three key sections: an overview of the historical background leading up to 1998, upon which the more concrete and procedural knowledge will sit; a content guidance section focusing on knowledge directly relevant to the specification; and an exam guidance section. The contents of these latter two are briefly summarised below.

The content guidance section is designed to clearly illustrate the required knowledge for this topic and is divided into four chapters that rigidly follow the needs of the specification. Each chapter is set out in a direct, student-friendly format with a clear building-block approach, starting with key roles, procedures and functions, then developing this with practical analysis of how things work in practice. In this way, analysis and evidence are built into each of the relevant chapters, helping students to identify the difference between knowledge and understanding and evaluation, and providing some examples for the points they wish to make.

Chapter 1 will focus on the four agreements since 1998 – Good Friday, St Andrews, Hillsborough and Stormont House – which effectively function as the 'constitution' for NI. Students should be aware that these documents dictate how NI government is supposed to operate. Chapters 2 and 3 will analyse and explore the operation of the Executive Committee and Assembly respectively, giving opportunities to explore how the two institutions interrelate. Chapter 4 will focus on the policies and development of the political parties and offer tentative conclusions as to why some parties are enjoying electoral success and others are not. In each of the chapters, key terms and concepts will be highlighted as appropriate, in order to enable students to build their political terminology as they progress through the book.

The final section will specifically address exam requirements and provide guidance on both exam preparation and how to approach individual questions. It will include insights into common mistakes and how to avoid them.

## Terminology

One of the key elements to studying a new discipline is learning language specific to that subject. Within this book are three aids for the acquisition of relevant political vocabulary: a guide to the abbreviations used, both within this book and in NI political life; a subject-specific glossary of terms; and relevant information boxes interwoven throughout the text, which place key terms alongside the appropriate context, enabling students to gradually increase their knowledge as they progress through the unit.

Students are encouraged to remember that they are studying, and therefore writing about, an academic subject, and to endeavour from the start to keep their writing precise and formal and to avoid using slang or colloquialisms, which may not be appropriate for a more developed academic study. In the context of NI politics, there are a few specific issues which need to be addressed, such as the use of the terms Catholic/Protestant, unionist/ nationalist; when and how to use abbreviations; and how to reference political leaders and groups. Although it is still not unusual for the NI conflict to be treated as religious-based and the terms Catholic/Protestant are often used colloquially to mean nationalist/unionist, political scientists do not endorse this approach. There are a number of theories regarding the nature of the divided society in NI and the dominant approach taken by political scientists is that NI is an example of an ethno-nationalist conflict made worse by the fact that the ethno-nationalist divisions also correspond with religious divisions. For this reason, more precise language should be used and, rather than referring to the two main communities as 'Catholic' and 'Protestant', the political terms 'nationalist' and 'unionist' are preferred.

In addition, it is important to recognise, where possible, the existence of other communities or identities. One of the criticisms that has been made of the agreements since 1998 is that they 'lock in' sectarianism by structuring the government around a power-sharing Executive based on two main political groups.[2] Sectarianism has been identified as one of the long-standing political and social problems in NI and could roughly be described as the tendency for citizens to identify with one of two main groups and to be unwilling to take seriously the views or beliefs of the other. At its worst this manifests itself in violence and public disorder but, in a lower scale, has resulted in segregated housing and education, particularly in more urban parts of NI. These groups are variously regarded as Catholic/ Protestant or unionist/nationalist, and sectarianism is attributed with being a key cause in violent attacks and continued hostility between the two sides of the community. As time has moved on, these two main groups continue to dominate the political landscape, however, there is increasing evidence of disruption to this pattern. The Green Party, for example, is beginning to gather momentum, and increasingly NI is starting to see political issues which fall completely outside the norm of nationalist/unionist politics. Like the Marriage (Same Sex Couples) Act 2013 – more commonly referred to as the 'Equal Marriage Act' – which, if applied to NI, would extend the right to marry to same sex couples. Therefore, while the political institutions continue to be dominated by unionist and nationalist parties, due attention does need to be given to other identities and groups.

With regard to the First Minister and deputy First Minister, it is important to recognise that the lower case 'd' at the start of 'deputy' is deliberate and reflects the fact that this is a joint Head of Executive role – a dyarchy – and that the two hold coequal powers. As elsewhere, abbreviations should be used correctly, with the full word being used on first usage and the abbreviations or acronyms thereafter. Students are advised to avoid abbreviating words such as 'parliament' or 'government', no matter how tempting this may be, especially in the context of an exam, as it is never acceptable in formal writing.

## Background

The devolution of some political power from Westminster to NI in 1998 (and in the series of agreements post 1998) is impossible to examine without making reference to the history of NI from 1920–98. However, the decision to include only a brief overview is a deliberate attempt to reinforce the fact that, while it is important for students to understand the historical background to the current political situation and arrangements, it is not a requirement of the specification that they should have a thorough knowledge of the pre-1998 era. What follows is, therefore, the briefest of scene-setting histories designed to establish the situation as it was at the signing of the Good Friday Agreement in 1998.

### 1920–1972

The Government of Ireland Act 1920 (Fourth Home Rule Bill) was an attempt to bring an end to the Anglo-Irish War, which was raging across Ireland at the time and bringing the British government more and more criticism both from within the British Isles and further afield. In an attempt to settle the 'Ulster question', it advocated a temporary partition of Ireland by establishing two Home Rule style parliaments: one in the new Northern Ireland to govern the northernmost six counties; and one in the South to establish a similar twenty-six-county dominion parliament. Although most northern unionists were happy with the act, southern unionists felt abandoned, whilst northern nationalists lived in hope for an end to what was seen as the absurdity of partition.

James Craig, enjoying a burgeoning Westminster career as a junior finance minister, reluctantly agreed to leave his London political life and return to NI to become the first NI prime minister. Elections were held and the first devolved Northern Irish government was set up. From the start, this was a government and state under pressure. A sizeable minority refused to recognise the state, hoping that it would be short lived, and were encouraged in this belief by the addition of a Boundary Commission to the 1921

Anglo-Irish Treaty, signed to end the war between the Irish Republican Army (IRA) and the British state.[3] The Boundary Commission was a device used by British Prime Minister David Lloyd George to deal with the 'Ulster question' during the treaty negotiations, and made provision for a border poll (to check how many people in NI wanted to remain part of Britain) to be held following the enactment of the treaty. The 1925 report which resulted from this recommended minor changes but, by mutual agreement, the Irish Free State and the NI government agreed to leave things as they were. However, the threat of the Boundary Commission, and the fear that it would lead to the loss of Fermanagh and Tyrone, caused considerable unionist anxiety in the interim and did not help the volatile situation in the new NI state. There was a pervasive sense of threat as successive unionist governments overestimated the influence of the Free State and believed all too readily its ostensibly all-Ireland rhetoric. This was exacerbated by the fear that the British government, even when Conservative, could not be trusted to stand up for unionist rights. These fears, accompanied by a long-standing ethnic division between nationalists and unionists in NI, and increasing violence in the north, led to a disastrous start for this new state, which was steeped in political violence and division from the start.

The unionist government, feeling insecure and threatened, and in reaction to concerns about the perceived nationalist threat, implemented a series of policies designed to strengthen their already dominant political position. For example, they abolished the use of proportional representation for local council elections in 1922, and for parliament itself in 1929. The implementation of a proportional voting system was seen as a way to ensure the fairest possible distribution of seats in the new NI parliament, and was therefore a way of safeguarding minority rights. However, it had always been difficult for unionists to accept, as it was regarded as un-British and unnecessary. Another measure used to bolster the unionist majority was the gerrymandering of electoral boundaries to create constituencies which would be more likely to return unionist MPs.[4] Likewise, in 1928 a company vote was introduced, whereby company owners received up to an additional six votes for each branch of their limited company. This disproportionately benefitted unionists since few nationalists owned limited companies. These measures not only increased the likelihood that unionists would remain in control, they were also an attempt to create a political system similar to the Westminster model.

Measures such as these ultimately led to a low-key but consistent discrimination against nationalists in housing allocation, employment and voting, with widespread statistical evidence supporting these allegations. However it is also worth noting that in nationalist-dominated councils there was also evidence of discrimination against unionists – an unfortunate indication that the entire NI system was guilty of discriminatory practices and suspicion, rather than just one part of it.[5]

In the 1960s came a civil rights campaign, heavily influenced by similar campaigns in America and elsewhere. With a focus on nationalist rights, it drew attention to areas in need of reform, using slogans such as 'One man one vote' in reference to the need for voting rights, and 'One family one house' in reference to alleged discrimination in the allocation of housing. Unionists suspected that republicans were using the civil rights movement to mobilise against the NI state, which resulted in a very different response to civil rights between the mainstream unionist and nationalist parts of the community. The British government was eventually forced to intervene, as civil rights marches increasingly came under attack, and eventually the movement gave rise to a crisis of legitimacy for the NI parliament in Stormont. The October 1968 civil rights riots sparked republican interest and republicans saw in this movement an opportunity for a fresh attempt to end partition. In this way, civil rights, political violence and the collapse of Stormont became intertwined.

The inability of the Stormont Executive to effectively deal with the escalating civil disorder, together with the attention of the world's media, put a question mark over the ability of the local assembly to deal effectively with the escalating political problem. The conflict (or what has euphemistically been called the 'Troubles') is generally regarded as having started in 1969, and by 1971 the situation was to become even more worrying.[6]

In August of that year, British Prime Minister Brian Faulkner introduced internment without trial, beginning with Operation Demetrius.[7] It was a drastic move, designed to try to deal with the security situation by arresting people (both republicans and loyalists) under suspicion of terrorism, and detaining them without trial. Such a policy is highly controversial in a democracy, since it breaks the rule of law but Faulkner had hoped that, having been used successfully in the late 1950s, internment would help to quell the growing violence. Instead it fuelled an already volatile situation and increased nationalist resentment towards the British state. The worsening security situation revived speculation that direct rule from Westminster was becoming more, rather than less likely.

In January 1972 came 'Bloody Sunday' when, during a civil rights march in Derry/Londonderry, the British army shot twenty-eight civilians, fourteen of whom died (thirteen immediately and one later).[8] In response, British Prime Minister Edward Heath, called for periodic border polls, all security matters to be transferred to Westminster and internment without trial to be phased out. When the Stormont Executive refused to cooperate, the UK government shut it down and instituted direct rule. On 30 March 1972, fifty-one years of self-rule was wrapped up in a thirty-hour debate in the House of Commons.

## 1972–1998

The following timeline shows the political responses to the situation in NI between the ending of Stormont rule in 1972 and the 1998 Good Friday Agreement. The focus is primarily on the actions taken by the UK government, so that the political road from 1972 to the signing of the Good Friday Agreement in 1998 can be clearly tracked. The more important or significant developments have been highlighted in bold and explained more fully, with a focus on political developments and attempts to resolve the NI situation. This has necessitated leaving out other significant events, specifically the numerous attacks by various militarised groups and the impact this had on all of the victims. This is in no way to diminish this aspect of the conflict, however, in the interest of meeting the specification needs as succinctly as possible, it was deemed inappropriate to go into detail on this aspect. Further information can be obtained from a number of sources detailed at the end of this book.

1973    **The Sunningdale Agreement**: Signed at Sunningdale Park in Berkshire in March 1973, this provided a blueprint for a 78-seat NI power-sharing Assembly with a Council of Ireland. The Council of Ireland was to be made up of representatives from the Irish parliament, Dáil Éireann (the Dáil) and the NI Executive. The agreement was to replace the suspended Stormont government, but was unable to command the level of support needed. The Social Democratic and Labour Party (SDLP), Alliance Party (APNI) and more moderate members of the Ulster Unionist Party (UUP) supported it, but many other UUP members were opposed, particularly to the Council of Ireland, which they saw as a dangerous institution that could lead to a united Ireland. The agreement contained many of the elements that would later be seen as an essential part of any future solution, for example, power sharing, an Irish dimension, guarantees for minority rights and proportional representation. It is generally accepted that it was too soon for a power-sharing Executive with an Irish dimension to be acceptable to unionists, particularly in the context of an ongoing IRA campaign. The activities of the IRA in this era, with 1972 and 1973 seeing particularly high levels of security force deaths, did not predispose the unionist community to support attempts at power sharing, and the Sunningdale Executive collapsed as a result of the Ulster Workers' Council strike in May 1974.[9]

**1975–6**  **Criminalisation, Ulsterisation, Normalisation**: 'Criminalisation' was a policy introduced by the British government in 1975 that aimed to represent the IRA as a criminal gang in order to undermine them. In practical terms, this resulted in the removal of the controversial Special Category status given to paramilitary prisoners and the building of a new conventional prison – the Maze prison, also commonly referred to as the 'H-blocks' due to the shape of its wings – to house these prisoners. 'Ulsterisation' made the Royal Ulster Constabulary (RUC) and the Ulster Defence Regiment (UDR)[10] primarily responsible for the security of NI, and in this way the role of the British army was to be reduced. 'Normalisation' was an attempt to present life in NI as normal as possible and resulted in the fast rebuilding of bombed buildings and speedy clean-up operations following terrorist attacks. This was all at considerable expense to the British government, yet the approach not only failed to resolve the security situation, it was to set the scene for the later hunger strikes, as it was during this era that the 'blanket protest' began.[11]

**1979**  **The Atkins Initiative**: Secretary of State Humphrey Atkins set up talks between the SDLP, the Democratic Unionist Party (DUP) and the Alliance Party to try and establish how devolution could be achieved in NI. The UUP refused to attend as they objected to the proposed discussion of an Irish dimension. The talks resulted in a UK government suggestion that devolution could go ahead with either a power-sharing Executive or majority rule. Nationalists and the Alliance Party rejected the majority rule option and unionists rejected power-sharing so it did not result in a new initiative. However, it did lay the groundwork for James Prior's attempt at devolution, which followed.

**1982**    **James Prior's 'Rolling Devolution':** James Prior succeeded Humphrey Atkins as secretary of state. In 1982, he suggested another attempt at devolution based on a 78-member assembly voted in by the single transferable vote system (STV). There was to be an Executive of 13 members. Elections were held, but the assembly never got off the ground, as nationalists refused to participate due to the lack of an Irish dimension. This was called 'rolling devolution' because the assembly was to have a consultative role only until power sharing could be agreed and then power would be devolved fully to NI, one department at a time.

**1985**    **The Anglo-Irish Agreement:** This was, by far, the most significant development since the implementation of direct rule, coming only a few years after the 1981 hunger strikes.[12] These had marked a significant turning point in the conflict and resulted in a number of important outcomes, including the rise in support for Sinn Féin who, by the 1983 Westminster General Election, had gained 13.4 per cent of the vote as compared to the SDLP's 17.9 per cent. This was an indication of the growing polarisation between the two main sides of the community and enhanced the belief that something needed to be done to prevent further deterioration of the security situation. The second consequence was the growing European and American criticism of the British government and its handling of the hunger strikes, as well as the escalating security situation in NI. This critique caused the UK government considerable embarrassment, and Margaret Thatcher was aware that her cabinet needed to come up with a new attempt to deal with the situation. The third consequence was a growing friendship and commitment between the Republic of Ireland (RoI) and the UK as a result of their working together at the EEC (now EU). This had led to the development of a much friendlier and cooperative stance on NI.[13] This last point was very significant, especially given the previously tense relationship between Britain and Ireland and their inability to see eye-to-eye on Northern Irish policy. Working together at the European level gave politicians and top civil servants of both jurisdictions a neutral space in which to discuss Northern Irish matters informally. This was to be a great help in moving the two countries to a joint approach, as happened with the Anglo-Irish Agreement.

The agreement was made up of thirteen articles in total and included provision for social justice measures, such as repeal of the 1954 Flags and Emblems (Display) Act (Northern Ireland). Its main content focused on stressing that unity would only be by consent of a majority in NI, but if a majority wanted unity the UK would not object. In practical terms, the setting up of North/South bodies in the form of the intergovernmental conference was a stealthy move. Infuriating to unionists, and of no real interest to nationalists, it established two very clear facts. Firstly, it established that unionists no longer had a veto over solutions in NI. Despite a long 'Ulster says No' campaign staged by unionists, and mainly aimed at the Intergovernmental Conference (IGC) the Conservative-led UK government held firm. Secondly it established the right of the British and Irish governments to act in the 'best interest' of NI over the heads of its citizens. Clearly, from 1985 onwards, some sort of an Irish dimension was a done deal. Both unionists and republicans disliked the Anglo-Irish Agreement, but there is no doubt that it set the stage for both groups reappraising their political stance, and eventually led to the Hume–Adams talks, which were an essential part of the road to peace.

1988     **John Hume and Gerry Adams talks:** SDLP leader John Hume initiated a series of talks with Sinn Féin leader Gerry Adams, hoping to persuade the IRA to give up arms.

1991     **Brooke Initiative:** In a speech in London in 1990, Peter Brooke (then secretary of state for Northern Ireland) stated that Britain had "no selfish strategic or economic interest" in NI and would not object to unification by consent. The following year he instigated a series of inter-party talks – later called the Brooke/Mayhew talks (in 1992, Sir Patrick Mayhew replaced Brooke as secretary of state) – attended by the UUP, the SDLP, the DUP and the Alliance Party. The purpose of the talks was to discuss the future of NI structured around three strands:

- Relationships within NI and how to achieve a devolved settlement
- Relations between NI and the RoI
- Relations between the British and Irish governments
- These talks ended in mid-July, but they had opened the door

for subsequent talks and behind-the-scenes negotiations, which continued throughout 1991 and 1992

1993     **Joint Declaration on Peace:** Also known as the **Downing Street Declaration**, this was issued by British Prime Minister John Major in conjunction with Irish Taoiseach Albert Reynolds. It was a nine-point document that appealed to both republican and loyalist paramilitaries to call ceasefires in return for a chance to negotiate a peaceful settlement. It clearly stated that a united Ireland would only happen if and when a majority of Northern Irish citizens wanted it, but it also made clear that, if negotiations were not successful, the British and Irish governments would work together to find a solution to the NI question. Initially unionists and republicans were sceptical about this and regarded it with suspicion. However, it was well supported by all the main British political parties and by the American administration, then led by President Clinton.

1994     **Paramilitary ceasefires:** on 31 August 1994, the IRA declared a 'complete' ceasefire, with the Combined Loyalist Military Command (CLMC) – an umbrella group for the Ulster Volunteer Force (UVF), the Ulster Defence Association (UDA) and the Red Hand Commando – following suit on 13 October.

1995     **Framework Documents released:** The Framework Documents were joint publications from the British and Irish governments stressing their commitment to peace in NI and to the consent principle. They emphasised the importance of self-determination and the need to end hostility in NI through democratic and imaginative means.

1996     **Peace talks begin:** The IRA ceasefire ended on 9 February 1996, when the Provisional IRA detonated a bomb in Canary Wharf, London. As a result of this, Sinn Féin were excluded from the peace talks that began later that year.

1997     **Upheaval in the peace talks:** In July, the IRA ceasefire was reinstated and, as a result, Sinn Féin were admitted back to the talks in August. This, however, caused the United Kingdom

Unionist Party (UKUP) and Democratic Unionist Party (DUP) to leave the talks in protest.

**1998**     **Good Friday Agreement**: This was signed on 10 April and put forward to the electorate of both NI and the Irish Republic for consent. On 22 May a referendum on the agreement was held with 71 per cent of the population voting in favour. It should be noted that unionists were less enthusiastic about the agreement than nationalists with approximately only 58 per cent of unionists voting in favour.

The purpose of this section is to set the scene for the development of devolution and to help explain how some of the key features of the new devolved institutions were devised. For example, the twin ideas of a power-sharing Executive and an Irish dimension had been mooted since 1973, but they emerged in one form or another in most of the serious attempts to resolve the issue. It is also fairly clear that the British government, while working to contain the situation when a solution seemed impossible, was always hoping for a return to devolution and was working towards that end.

From 1969 to 1998 there were 3,636 deaths as a direct result of the actions of the military wings of loyalism, republicanism and the British security forces. The Northern Ireland Office estimate that approximately 500,000 people in NI have been directly and adversely affected by the conflict. As it stands just under 500 people are currently living with life-altering physical injuries and, as the definition of 'victim' is still subject to political debate, some of these people do not receive pensions or the means to make up for their loss of income. WAVE trauma centre, working in conjunction with medical and other academics, have identified ongoing transgenerational issues as a result of the conflict, namely higher levels of drug and alcohol abuse, higher levels of suicide and lower life expectancy rates. The conflict in NI had a deeply traumatic effect on the entire community and many aspects of that are only now, tentatively being examined.

The agreements detailed in the next chapter were designed to provide the blueprint for a new political system that would move NI forward and away from those dark days of conflict.

**Endnotes**

1  The term Good Friday Agreement is the one used throughout this book. For clarity, students should be aware that if they come across the term 'Belfast Agreement' in their wider reading, it refers to the same document.

2 Taylor, Rupert, ed. *Consociational Theory: McGarry and O'Leary and the Northern Ireland Conflict*, (Routledge, 2009). This book was structured around a discussion between leading academic supporters of the consociational model used in NI and those who felt it was inappropriate precisely because it based the political system and institutions on the sectarian divisions that had caused the trouble in the first place. It is not the only account of this criticism of the Good Friday Agreement but it is one of the clearest.

3 This earlier organisation should not be confused with the more modern IRA, as the earlier movement was concerned with achieving independence from Britain and was considerably different to the organisation which emerged in the 1960s, focused on NI and the desire to end partition.

4 The term 'gerrymandering' was first used in an 1812 article in the *Boston Gazette* that criticised nineteenth-century governor of Massachusetts, Elbridge Gerry, and his redrawing of district boundaries in a way that guaranteed favourable election results. The article drew attention in particular to one boundary that resembled a salamander.

5 John McGarry and Brendan O'Leary in *Explaining Northern Ireland: Broken Images* (Wiley, 1995), attest that there was evidence of nationalist councils discriminating against unionists but that it was not on the same scale as unionist discrimination against nationalists, nor was it as frequently noted.

6 As is the case with many historical events, the precise starting date for the conflict is a matter for debate and is equally highly politicised. Some argue that it began in 1966 when a revised version of the Ulster Volunteer Force (UVF) emerged, carrying out three attacks on Catholics in Belfast and resulting in the deaths of three people, Matilda Gould, John Scullion and Peter Ward.

7 A detailed and analytical account of Operation Demetrius can be found in McCleery, Martin, *Operation Demetrius and its aftermath: A new history of the use of internment without trial in Northern Ireland 1971–75* (Manchester University Press, 2015).

8 The events of this day were subjected to two public inquiries, including one of the most extensive and expensive inquiries carried out in Britain, the 2010 Saville Inquiry, which took 12 years and cost £195 million.

9 This strike was not sanctioned by the main trade unions and was actively discouraged by numerous trade union officials who saw it as divisive and contrary to union guidelines.

10 A branch of the British army based in NI and mostly composed of part-time members drawn from the local, and predominantly Protestant, community. It was later renamed the Royal Irish Regiment (RIR). During the conflict, 264 members lost their lives.

11 Some republican prisoners, in response to the denial of Special Category status, refused to wear prison uniform or to adhere to normal prison discipline. By 1980 there were approximately 400 prisoners on the 'blanket protest' in both the Maze prison and Armagh women's jail.

12 On 1 March 1981, on the fifth anniversary of the ending of special category status, a string of selected IRA volunteer prisoners instituted a hunger strike in the Maze prison, demanding that political status for paramilitary prisoners be reinstated. By the time the strike had ended, on 3 October 1981, ten men had died as a result of the protest.

13 This has been noted in numerous studies such as that by Katy Hayward, *Irish Nationalism and European Integration: The official redefinition of the island of Ireland,* (Manchester University Press, 2009).

# THE FOUR AGREEMENTS

# 1998–2014
# The Four Agreements: The Constitutional Framework for Northern Ireland

This chapter will briefly outline the content of the four main agreements which, taken together, form the blueprint for the operation of devolution in NI. These four agreements – the Good Friday Agreement 1998; St Andrews 2007; Hillsborough 2010; and Stormont House 2014 – in conjunction with the Northern Ireland Act 1998, act as the constitution for the devolved institutions and lay out how the political system should work. By far the most important is the Good Friday Agreement, and it will therefore be assigned the greatest attention. For each agreement, the focus will be on how it came about and what specific change it brought to the political system. Where appropriate, there will be some brief discussion of the reaction of the various parties and political groups. It is important to have an understanding of these four agreements but it is not likely that questions in the exam would focus directly on the agreements or expect detailed knowledge of their contents. This chapter also presents some key political concepts which are necessary for all students to understand, and which form an important part of the political vocabulary and analysis of this unit. To this end, the chapter explores how NI was governed under direct rule and outlines a key political concept – the 'democratic deficit'.

There had been a number of attempted solutions to the NI conflict between 1972 and 1998 but, for one reason or another, all had failed. However by the mid-1990s, not only had the political environment shifted enough to allow for a new attempt at peace, but certain key individuals came to the fore at this time, dedicated to finding a lasting solution. One of these was the Conservative Prime Minister John Major, who began the process completed by Tony Blair's Labour government.

Both Major and Blair understood what other British prime ministers had apparently failed to grasp – that, for peace to be achieved, they needed to dedicate considerable time and resources to developing a lasting solution. They, like all parties involved, would have to be absolutely determined not to give up, that finding an acceptable solution must be made a priority.

Ultimately it was to be Blair's government – following Labour's landslide victory in the 1997 British general election – that was credited with bringing peace to NI, and Blair went on to have a career working in conflict resolution in the Middle East, largely on the basis of the experience he gained while negotiating the Good Friday Agreement. Like John Major, he displayed a focus, determination and willingness to try new solutions, all of which were needed to help achieve the settlement eventually signed in April 1998.

Bill Clinton's American administration was especially keen to support any attempt at a solution, and Clinton helped by offering the services of Senator George Mitchell as diplomat, who kept the momentum of the talks going at critical times, when it looked like things could grind to a halt. Mitchell has retained strong links with NI.

All of these individuals played a key role in the events that shaped the peace negotiations and the Good Friday Agreement itself, and are therefore worthy of mention.

## What inspired the Good Friday Agreement?

As discussed, the Good Friday Agreement was largely a result of changing political circumstances, including a change in the relationship between the British and Irish governments. The SDLP promoted the idea that for there to be any chance of peace, Sinn Féin needed to be involved in dialogue, and a solution had to be found which would appeal to republicans as much as any other group in NI. This was difficult for the British government and unionist groups to accept, but ultimately a willingness to try was imperative for progress to be made.

By 1991, it was clear that, for all parties in NI, Britain and Ireland, it was no longer acceptable to simply manage the situation in NI. Rather, the situation had to end. Internationally, the end of the Cold War meant that there was no longer any strategic need for Britain to hold on to NI. While the Cold War had been ongoing, NI had provided an important base for NATO forces, should they be needed, and once it ended, those bases became less important and the strategic location of NI less significant. Meanwhile, the fall of apartheid in South Africa seemed to offer hope that even the most bitterly divided society could find peace.

In addition, there was growing criticism of the simply undemocratic nature of direct rule. Technically, NI may well have been "as British as

Finchley", as noted by Margaret Thatcher in 1981, but when you stripped away the rhetoric and looked at how laws were actually made for NI, there was a significant difference between it and the rest of the UK. One of the main inspirations behind the Good Friday Agreement was the desire to end this 'democratic deficit'.

The combination of a willingness by all the main political actors, including the British and Irish governments, a changing international situation, and a belief that the 'temporary' period of direct rule really needed to come to an end, all contributed to the development of the Good Friday Agreement.

## Direct rule and the 'democratic deficit'

The introduction outlined the attempted solutions to the NI conflict between 1972 and 1998. However, the detail of how NI was actually governed during this time was not examined. This section examines the arguments in favour of and against direct rule and considers why some academics and political commentators, such as Arthur Aughey and Duncan Morrow, would suggest that the methods for making laws for NI under direct rule were not sufficiently democratic, giving rise to the allegation of a democratic deficit.

The term 'direct rule' in NI's case suggested that the region would be ruled in exactly the same way as the rest of the UK, so that the worst that could happen would be a lack of regional-specific laws. Indeed, there is still an argument, often used by the regions in the north of England and in Scotland, that laws made at Westminster fail to take into consideration the needs of the regions – indeed, this is one of the arguments being used in favour of devolution for both Wales and Scotland – and is one way that direct rule can be seen as an unsatisfactory form of democratic rule.

However, objections to NI direct rule are based on much more than this. Under direct rule, NI was governed in a uniquely different manner to the rest of Britain – a problem described as democratic deficit. Under direct rule, power was concentrated in the hands of the secretary of state for NI, a full British cabinet minister who ruled in conjunction with a number of junior ministers, each of whom represented mainland British constituencies. Essentially the role of Secretary of State is to exercise executive power – the power to suggest policies and maintain the day-to-day running of the province – along with drafting policy initiatives and keeping within required budgets.

The secretary of state, especially in his/her first few months in power, will, due to their higher level of local knowledge, rely heavily on the Head of the Civil Service in NI for advice and guidance on a range of matters, such as how to allocate resources and implement policy. The secretary of state would frequently defer to their expertise, giving them a lot of hidden power. Sir Patrick Mayhew described his time as secretary of state (1992–97) as not unlike that of a colonial governor, with few restrictions on what he could do or suggest as policy for NI.

The secretary of state, like the prime minister in Britain, also had access to a wide range of patronage powers. This, too, was criticised. When Stormont was suspended in 1972, the local councils were stripped of their powers. Quangos (organisations that carried out some government functions) were set up to do work previously done by the councils, and the members of these were appointed directly by the secretary of state and the junior ministers. After the signing of the Anglo-Irish Treaty in 1985, Dublin was given limited say in the allocation of some quango posts, however, this was still a very undemocratic way for public posts to be allocated. Both the method of appointment for quangos and the lack of accountability for their decisions were central features of the democratic deficit.

## KEY TERMS

**Secretary of state** – official title of any cabinet minister appointed by the prime minister. Therefore, the secretary of state for NI is the cabinet minister responsible for NI. Like any other cabinet minister, they are expected to make sure their department, in this case NI, is well-run, sticks to government budgets and is generally in keeping with government policy.

**Executive power** – the power to suggest laws and to come up with a programme for government.

**Patronage** – the power of appointment. It can include a large number of appointments. For example, the British prime minister can appoint cabinet members amongst other posts. It is a useful power as it can be used to reward loyalty, to gain support or to silence opponents.

**Accountability** – one of the key ways democracy is maintained is by making sure public officials are held accountable. There need to be methods in place to ensure that they are behaving appropriately, spending public money correctly and adhering to the rule of law.

**Legislative power** – the power to pass laws. Usually in a democracy this is a power belonging to an elected assembly or parliament.

The democratic deficit also applies to how laws for NI were made under direct rule. In fact, for most analysts, this is the focus of the complaint that direct rule is an unfair and undemocratic system. The first thing that needs to be understood is that the act that dealt with the suspension of Stormont in 1972 was called the Temporary Provisions Act and it was, as the name suggests, intended to be only a short-term measure with a new NI parliament set up as soon as possible. For the British government, direct rule was only supposed to last a short time. This partly explains why the arrangements for law making in NI were so unsatisfactory – they were only supposed to cover a few months until things settled down and a new arrangement could be worked out.

Under the Temporary Provisions Act, legislation for NI was passed through Orders in Council, a method usually reserved for passing statutory instruments or secondary legislation at Westminster. However, since Orders do not go through the same rigorous stages as a normal bill this is seen as a notoriously undemocratic method for passing laws. There is, for example, no line-by-line consideration of wording, and Orders are not subject to the usual debates, or back-and-forth scrutiny between the two Houses of Parliament. As a result, MPs cannot suggest amendments, and can only vote against or in favour of the Order (i.e. a straight vote).

During this time, NI legislation originated with the NI Office, essentially coming directly from the secretary of state who was acting on agreed government policy. As amendments could not be made, legislation for NI received less legislative scrutiny than that for Britain as a whole. Few MPs other than NI MPs attended the vote for the Orders in Council – which are also voted on late at night when attendance at the Commons is already low – and so these passed without challenge. The system was, in fact, akin to having the secretary of state rule by decree.

A further criticism of direct rule was the basic lack of accountability. One of the safeguards in a democratic system is the ability for the Executive to be held to account. In British politics there are several ways for this to happen: Prime Minister's Questions, written questions, select committee enquiries, debates, and Lords Questions. However, under direct rule, the main form of accountability was the monthly Question Time at Westminster. After the establishment of the NI Affairs Select Committee, which was only set up in 1993, things were marginally better. However, even taken together, these two opportunities for scrutiny could not be seen as enough to ensure adequate accountability.

However, it must be remembered that direct rule also has some positive points and there are arguments in favour as well as against. For many years some unionists (DUP included) saw direct rule as a better option than power sharing. There was also a recent upsurge in calls for a return to direct rule following the Renewable Heat Incentive (RHI) scandal, and the resultant political impasse and general feeling of discontent at the inability of the Executive to come to a political agreement. Frustration amongst the electorate at frequent disruptions to the operation of politics, the inability of politicians from the bigger parties to set aside differences and work cooperatively, and the intractable problem of dealing with legacy issues has given support to the view that direct rule might be better.

## LEARNING OPPORTUNITY

**Students should write a page explaining what is meant by the term 'democratic deficit'. They should include information on who suggested laws, how they were passed and what type of scrutiny there was during direct rule.**

| Arguments in favour of direct rule for NI |
|---|
| 1. It limits the scope for sectarianism to influence decisions – especially since, in 1985, the RoI was co-opted to act as guarantor of nationalist rights. |
| 2. Direct rule ministers are accountable through ministerial Question Time and the NI Affairs Select Committee. |
| 3. It guarantees a more stable government than devolution, with little scope for suspensions or inability to deal with issues because of lack of cooperation. |
| 4. It guarantees a common set of standards across the UK, with regard to areas such as housing, health and education. |
| 5. It is a way of making sure that NI is always governed (avoiding those periods of political inactivity that have sometimes occurred at Stormont during devolution). |
| 6. It is seen by some in NI, specifically integrationist unionists, as a way to secure the union. |

**Arguments against direct rule for NI**

1. The democratic deficit – devolved government is arguably more effective because locally-elected politicians are more responsive to the needs of the region than ministers under direct rule.

2. Direct rule allows laws to be made in an unaccountable and highly discredited manner using Orders in Council. Devolution allows for a more open and accountable process for law making.

3. Despite the existence of the NI Affairs Select Committee, many argue that there is not enough detailed scrutiny of direct rule ministers.

4. Direct rule prevents local politicians from developing a sense of responsibility, since they are not involved in decision-making.

5. Some unionists believe that direct rule itself could be a bigger threat to the union as it would give Westminster complete control over NI.

6. Some nationalists believe that direct rule will take them further away from a united Ireland.

## The Good Friday Agreement, 1998

### A consociational model

The Good Friday Agreement provided a consociational model for the new devolved government. This is a democratic system specifically designed to provide a workable and lasting democracy in a divided society, where it is recognised that there may need to be special provisions for democracy to work. It was regarded as the best option for NI and was a development of previous attempts at power sharing with an Irish dimension. The form of consociationalism brought in by the agreement can best be seen as consociational with external elements.

The four key features of consociationalism:

1. **Power sharing** – there must be a power-sharing coalition government to make sure that both communities have a role in government.
2. **A proportional electoral system** – to try to guarantee as fair representation of all communities as possible. Proportionality should also be seen in the allocation of public expenditure and public office.
3. **Segmental autonomy** – cultural equality.
4. **Mutual veto** – a method to make sure that important legislation either has the support of both communities or it cannot go through.

How does the Good Friday Agreement fulfil these four criteria?

**Power sharing**
- Originally the Executive Committee was made up of a twelve-member, four-party coalition. Restructuring of the Executive in 2014 resulted in a reduction in the number of executive departments from twelve to nine.

- The relationship between the Executive and the Assembly.

- The intra-assembly relations among parties, particularly among Statutory Committees (see Chapter 3).

**Proportionality**
- STV/proportional representation system of election for the local assembly (see Chapter 4).

- Use of the D'Hondt rule (see Chapter 2) to appoint all members of the Executive, allocate committee chairs and deputy chairs, and compose the Statutory Committees.

**Segmental autonomy**
- Creation of the Equality Commission and a range of new equality laws have guaranteed segmental autonomy.

- The right of all citizens in NI to self-designate as either British or Irish.

**Mutual veto**
- By using weighted majority or parallel consent in legislative votes in the Assembly.

- Petitions of concern (see Chapter 3).

- Mutual veto in the North South Ministerial Council (NMSC) decisions.

- Mutual veto in key decisions within the Executive, for example, in formulating the budget or the Programme for Government.

Of these, probably the best known are the use of petitions of concern and the use of weighted majority voting in the Assembly. These will be considered more fully in the section on the working of the Assembly (see Chapter 3).

*LEARNING OPPORTUNITY*

Students should discuss why these features would be helpful in a divided society. The class could be broken into groups, with each group taking one feature and reporting back to the whole class on its conclusions

### Confirmation of the consent principle

The Good Friday Agreement was designed to replace both the Anglo-Irish Agreement 1985 and the Government of Ireland Act 1920. It began by addressing constitutional issues and very clearly stated that the future status of NI was entirely in the hands of the NI electorate. This confirmation of the 'consent principle' was required to settle unionist fears that this agreement was an attempt to manoeuvre them into joint authority, without their express consent. It also stated that if, at a future date (for it recognised that at the time of publication in 1998 it was clear that the majority in NI wanted to remain part of Britain), there was a majority in favour of a united Ireland, then the British government would duly put this into law without further debate. Finally, one of the most innovative and groundbreaking aspects of the agreement was that it allowed NI citizens to identify as British or Irish, or both. As laid out in Section 1 clause (vi), the two governments:

> *Recognise the birth right of all the people of Northern Ireland to identify themselves and be accepted as Irish or British, or both, as they may so choose, and accordingly confirm that their right to hold both British and Irish citizenship is accepted by both Governments and would not be affected by any future change in the status of NI.*

This was reinforced by having further safeguards for both communities from external bodies, as found in strands 2 and 3:

**Strand 1** lays out the guidelines for the democratic devolved institutions in NI.

**Strand 2 – North–South Ministerial Council (NSMC)** – deals with relations within the island of Ireland. The British and Irish governments saw the NSMC as an extension of the IGC, which was set up as part of the Anglo-Irish Agreement. Nationalists saw this as a potential lead-in to an all-Ireland – a view shared by unionists, causing them to view this body with great suspicion.

The NSMC was also seen as a way of further guaranteeing minority rights by giving a discrete forum where minority rights issues could be raised, if required, during the twice-yearly plenary sessions, or at any of the smaller, more frequent meetings held throughout the year.

**Strand 3 – British–Irish Council** – deals with relations within the British Isles, more commonly known as 'East–West relations'. In the context of a new devolved Britain, this allowed for the devolved institutions of all regions within the UK, along with the Irish government, to come together to discuss matters of common concern which would frequently relate to EU matters. This was seen as making devolution more palatable to unionists, who had always had difficulty with what they regarded as an 'un-British' form of democracy. The extension of devolution to both Scotland and Wales removed some of this sense of loss of British identity, and the provision for a specifically British forum went some way to further easing concerns unionists had about some aspects of the agreement, such as power sharing and the NSMC.

The need for safeguards to meet the requirements of both parts of the community is a central theme throughout the agreement, and is also evidenced in the sections on rights, decommissioning, security, policing and justice, and prisoners. These sections reflect the various interests and requirements of the main negotiating partners and, in some respects, illuminate the compromises made in order to get the Good Friday Agreement signed.

The focus in this book will be on the operation of devolution, as laid out in Strand 1, and reference will be made to the other sections, as and when appropriate. The original agreement is available online from CAIN (the Conflict Archive on the Internet based at the University of Ulster), and it is highly recommended as a primary source.

## Strand 1 – The democratic institutions in Northern Ireland

In this section, the aim is to gain a sound overview of the core mechanisms or procedures set out by the Agreement, as it provides the blueprint for the governing of NI. More detailed aspects of these provisions will be dealt with in the relevant chapters on the operation of devolution.

The Assembly is described as the prime authority on all devolved responsibilities, reflecting the tradition of parliamentary sovereignty within the British system. This is the main legislative body and, in keeping with the parliamentary tradition, it has three main functions:

- the passing of legislation
- representing the wishes of the electorate and relevant political parties
- scrutiny of the Executive

In Chapter 3, these functions will be analysed in more detail, but it is useful to remember these three main roles while examining the provisions laid down by the Good Friday Agreement.

It was set up to have 108 members, to be called Members of the Legislative Assembly or MLA for short, all elected by a proportional representation method known as the single transferable vote (PR-STV). Within the Agreement, there are a number of safeguards (noted at the start of the section on the Assembly) designed to prevent any dominance by one community over the other. These include the following:

1. The provision that all committee chairs, ministers and committee members be allocated according to party strength, in some cases by the implementation and use of the D'Hondt formula (see page 55).
2. The incorporation of the European Convention on Human Rights into the legal system and the setting up of a Human Rights Commission.
3. The suggestion that NI should have its own separate bill of rights, and that time should be spent devising this.
4. The provision that key decisions will be: a) checked to ensure they do not infringe on rights; and b) taken on a cross-community basis, using either parallel consent or a weighted majority. It is therefore important to define what constitutes a key decision. These can either be identified in advance or designated as such following the, often controversial (as will be seen later in the book), 'Petition of Concern' veto – a parliamentary procedure wherein a group of at least thirty or more MLAs can block a decision made by the Assembly by requiring a show of cross-community support. At the very first meeting of the Assembly, MLAs were required to designate as unionist, nationalist or 'other'. Some saw this as setting the sectarian divide in stone, but it was in fact a necessary part of the provisions for taking key decisions, as these designations would then be used to ascertain community support in such votes.

While most of the safeguarding measures are unique to the system of democracy developed in NI, and reflect its unique history, the remaining features are more familiar, regular features of a democratic system.

Each of the Executive branches or departments was designed to have a Statutory Committee. These committees are the powerhouse of the Assembly and are designed to do three things:

1. scrutinise the work of the department and the minister
2. act as a consultative body and work with the minister
3. initiate policy and relevant reports for that area of government

The chairs and deputy chairs of these committees are appointed using the D'Hondt principle, and must be from an opposing party to the minister in charge of the department. Although it is expected that the minister and committee will work together, it is also expected that the committee will challenge the minister when appropriate. There is also a provision in the Agreement for special committees to be set up to check if a measure or a proposed bill conforms to equality requirements. This can happen as a result of a request by the Executive Committee or by the relevant Statutory Committee.

It is the job of the Assembly to pass primary legislation. Bills originate from the relevant minister, committee or from individual MLAs (Private Members' Bills) and are passed on the basis of a simple majority vote, unless they need cross-community support. One of the quirks in the legislative provisions is the ability of the Assembly to pass legislation on reserved matters "with the approval of the Secretary of State and subject to parliamentary control". The 'parliament' referred to here is the Westminster Parliament, not the Assembly. This is an unusual power, which obviously gives scope for the legislative authority in the Assembly to be extended and stretched to cover areas that, strictly speaking, are no longer the remit of Westminster. This power has been used and several bills have been passed using this method.

Clause 33 in the Agreement refers to the role of Westminster with regard to the devolved institutions and governance of NI. In this, the right of the Assembly to legislate on reserved matters, if support from both the Secretary of State and Westminster Parliament is given, is again reiterated. This emphasises the extent to which the Westminster government is keen to see the NI institutions assume as much legislative power as possible, and to provide ways to avoid the use of Orders in Council when passing legislation for NI. In short, this allows Westminster to allocate discretionary powers to the Assembly when dealing with reserved matters.

## The Executive Committee and the role of ministers

The Executive Committee was given the power of Executive authority and the precise clauses dealing with this can be found between clauses 10 and 26 in the agreement. Originally the Executive was a team of ten ministers, each in charge of a devolved department, and with a corresponding Statutory Committee to both assist and monitor them, headed by a dyarchy consisting of the First Minister and deputy First Minister (twelve ministers in total).[1] The First Minister and deputy First Minister were originally to be elected by the Assembly voting on a cross-community basis, with the proviso that one must be from the unionist and one from the nationalist political groupings. However, this has emerged to be a foregone conclusion, with the leader of the biggest party, following an election, taking up post as First Minister, and the leader of the largest party of the opposing community taking up office as deputy First Minister. These roles where designed to be coequal and they have a joint support office (rather like the Prime Minister's Office in the UK system). Until 2016 they were known as the Office of the First Minister and deputy First Minister, or the OFMdFM for short, but in 2016 the new name of Executive Office was adopted. The ministerial posts are allocated using the D'Hondt method to keep the process as fair and equitable as possible.

The architects of the Agreement expected that ministers would take the initiative in their area of responsibility, much more so than is the case, for example, in the UK system. This is reinforced by a clause stating that ministers will have full Executive authority in their respective areas of responsibility. The lack of collective responsibility in the Executive Committee, alongside this very forthright statement of ministerial power, did give rise to some problems with so-called 'solo runs' (see page 59), which required tightening up in the St Andrews Agreement.

The last clause in this section, clause 25, reinforces the need for a complete commitment to non-violence. It states: "Those who hold office should use only democratic, non-violent means and those who do not should be excluded or removed from office under these provisions." This clause is one of many small additions to the document intended to allay the fears of both communities.

Clause 34 stated that the secretary of state for NI would be responsible for matters not devolved to the Assembly and for representing the interests of NI in the UK cabinet. It also allowed for the setting up of an innovative body – the Civic Forum – which ran from 2000–2, but was not convened during the period of suspension, nor after devolution was restored following the St Andrews Agreement.

**Main features of the Good Friday Agreement**

1. A three-stranded approach to deliver peace: strand one to focus on the devolved institutions in NI; strand two to deal with North–South cooperation; and strand three to set up procedures for East–West cooperation.

2. Strand 1 set out the details for the operation of a regional devolved parliament in NI.

3. This parliament was to be elected using PR-STV and to have 108 MLAs.

4. It was to be headed by an Executive Committee (equivalent to the Cabinet in the UK system) and a First Minister and deputy First Minister.

5. The Executive Committee would have responsibility for suggesting new laws, running the country on a day-to-day basis and spending the budget allocation wisely.

6. The First Minister and deputy First Minister roles were coequal: one cannot exist without the other.[2]

7. The Assembly has the normal powers associated with a parliament, i.e. to legislate, scrutinise the Executive and to represent their parties and the electorate.

8. The Assembly has a range of powers at their disposal to carry out these roles.

9. Only matters that are devolved or transferred can be legislated for at Stormont, other matters remain under the control of Westminster.

10. There are safeguards built into the system, reflecting the consociational model of democracy, to make sure that both sides of the community feel protected and listened too. For example, the requirement for cross-community voting on key decisions.

11. There are a number of additional matters that were reformed in order to allow the peace process to progress. These include the early release of prisoners, the reform of the RUC into a more inclusive police force, the PSNI and plans for decommissioning of all paramilitary weapons.

## Powers available to the NI Assembly and Executive

| Devolved Powers | Excepted Powers | Reserved Powers |
|---|---|---|
| Transferred matters for which the Assembly has full control | Matters of national importance and therefore under the control of the UK government | Issues where the NI Assembly can legislate with the consent of the UK government through the Secretary of State |
| • Health and social services<br>• Education<br>• Employment and skills<br>• Agriculture<br>• Social security<br>• Pensions and child support<br>• Housing<br>• Economic development<br>• Local government<br>• Environmental issues, including planning<br>• Transport<br>• Culture and sport<br>• NI civil service<br>• Equality<br>• Policing and justice (as of 2010) | • The UK constitution<br>• Royal succession<br>• International relations<br>• Defence and the armed forces<br>• Nationality, immigration and asylum<br>• Elections<br>• National security<br>• Nuclear energy<br>• UK-wide taxation<br>• Currency<br>• Conferring of honours<br>• International treaties | • Firearms and explosives<br>• Financial services and pension regulation<br>• Broadcasting<br>• Import and export controls<br>• Navigation and civil aviation<br>• International trade and financial markets<br>• Telecommunications and postage<br>• The foreshore and seabed<br>• Disqualification from Assembly membership<br>• Consumer safety |

## From referendum to renegotiation: 1998–2002

The Good Friday Agreement would not succeed without public support so, on 22 May 1998, two referenda were held in both the RoI and in NI. The referendum in the RoI was primarily to obtain support for the removal of Articles 2 and 3 of the Irish constitution – a source of discontent for unionists since their inception in 1937. These articles laid claim to NI, and their removal was a vital part of securing unionist support for the Agreement. Although unionists remained sceptical about the real intentions of the Irish government, and continued to see the Irish state as a threat, they could take some consolation from the 94.4 per cent of people in RoI who gave support for the referendum.

In the corresponding NI referendum, the electorate was asked to vote in favour of, or against, the provisions of the Agreement, a copy of which had been sent to every household in NI in preparation for the vote. A high turnout of 81 per cent, with a 71 per cent 'Yes' vote in favour of the devolved institutions, seemed to bode well. However, on further analysis, it became clear that there was more support for the Agreement from the nationalist community (99 per cent) than from unionists (57 per cent) and there was therefore more support from one side of the communal divide than from the other, indicating difficult times ahead.

Unionist apprehensions became apparent nearly immediately when, the day after the referenda were held, the *Belfast News Letter* carried the headline "Trimble facing revolt" – a reference to the then leader of the Ulster Unionist Party (UUP) and soon-to-be first ever First Minister, David Trimble, who was already facing problems keeping his party united and behind the Agreement. Six of the ten UUP Westminster MPs were against it; and one, Peter Weir, eventually left the UUP to join the DUP – the DUP had refused to even take part in the negotiations, instead providing strong opposition from outside the gates of Stormont during talks. The 'No' campaign in opposition to the Agreement included the DUP, UKUP, and three high-profile UUP Westminster MPs – Willie Ross, Willie Thompson and Roy Beggs. As noted by political scientist, Fearghal Cochrane, "The most interesting aspect of what was quite a coordinated and slick campaign was that virtually none of it focused on the central political architecture of the Good Friday Agreement".[3]

The main areas for concern for unionists were:
1. They thought it would destroy the union with Britain.
2. It would allow Sinn Féin into government before decommissioning of arms took place.
3. It would allow for the early release of prisoners.
4. It had provisions for future reform of the RUC and the creation of a new policing service.

In addition to unionist opponents, a negligible number of hard-core republicans were also anti-Agreement. On 15 August 1998, before the Agreement even got underway, dissident republicans carried out one of the worst atrocities of the Troubles, the Omagh bomb. Exploding in the town centre on a busy shopping day, the bomb killed twenty-nine people and two unborn babies, injuring over two hundred others. What was different about this bomb was the condemnation it brought from all sides – a glimmer of hope that things had really changed.

Once the referenda results were in, plans moved ahead for setting up the new institutions with the first ever Assembly elections being held in June 1998. Decommissioning was proving to be a huge stumbling block and led to increasing delays; for a year, the main unionist and nationalist parties argued about what the Agreement said about this issue. In an attempt to move things along, the British government set an arbitrary deadline of 30 June 1999 for the establishment of the first Executive Committee. This was moved back to 15 July 1999, but on that date, as nominations for ministerial posts in the Executive Committee were about to take place, the UUP, in a desperate attempt to retain their support, refused to nominate. The DUP and Alliance also refused to nominate, which led to the farcical situation of the SDLP and Sinn Féin holding all of the ministerial posts for ten minutes until the whole process was suspended, pending review by Senator George Mitchell. In fact, the first Executive was not formed until 29 November 1999, with David Trimble as First Minister and Seamus Mallon as deputy First Minister. This was only possible because Trimble got agreement from his party to take the UUP into government without decommissioning having taken place. He did, however, agree that if there was not substantial decommissioning by February 2000, he would withdraw the UUP and effectively collapse the Executive.

Power was devolved to NI on 1 December 1999. It appeared to be doomed from the start. David Trimble presided over a split party, which he was rapidly losing control of; and Ian Paisley, leader of the DUP, made the most of every opportunity to undermine him. By February, in anticipation of Trimble being forced to pull out of the Executive, the then secretary of state, Peter Mandelson, suspended devolution. The devolved institutions had lasted 72 days.

Devolution was restored in May 2000, but by this stage, Trimble's days as party leader were numbered, as support for the UUP ebbed away. This period saw a vicious loyalist feud develop between the Ulster Volunteer Force (UVF) and Ulster Freedom Fighters (UFF), and then another between the UVF and Loyalist Volunteer Force (LVF). Loyalist shootings rose from thirty-three in 1998 to one hundred and twenty-four in 2001–2.

Other events only served to increase tension and add to the sense that the Agreement was never going to work. From June–November 2001, in an incident that drew worldwide censure, loyalists picketed the Catholic

Holy Cross primary school, shouting sectarian abuse, throwing projectiles at the schoolchildren and their parents, and claiming that Catholics had been attacking their homes and denying them access to facilities.

In October 2002, things got much worse when the security forces alleged that an IRA spy ring was operating out of Stormont. Denis Donaldson, head of Sinn Féin's administration, was arrested and accused of possessing documents likely to be of use to terrorists.[4] The UUP reacted to what was dubbed 'Stormontgate', by threatening to withdraw from the Executive if Sinn Féin were not removed from office, and the British government once again suspended devolution on 14 October 2002.

## The St Andrews Agreement, 2007

Feargal Cochrane notes, "The whole structure of politics in NI changed between 2002 and 2007, as did the personalities at the top."[5] By 2003, the biggest party in NI was the DUP, having overtaken the UUP as the largest unionist party, as discontent amongst unionists regarding some aspects of the Agreement had rumbled on.[6]

The DUP had also changed policy from its earlier position of wrecking the Agreement from within – they had frequently rotated DUP ministers and refused to cooperate with the NSMC – and now favoured a renegotiation of the original Agreement. Similarly by 2003, Sinn Féin had eclipsed the SDLP. At first, this seemed to signal disaster for the future of devolution, but it soon became clear that both of these parties were ready to move on and were possibly more likely to deliver a lasting agreement than their more moderate counterparts.

By 2004, both the DUP and Sinn Féin were eager to get into government. For the DUP the main issue was that of decommissioning, and for Sinn Féin it was gaining an amnesty for 'on-the-runs' – republicans suspected of, but never charged for, terrorist crimes – and full implementation of the Good Friday Agreement. The post-9/11 international political environment meant that the US administration was less tolerant of Irish republicanism, which added pressure on Sinn Féin. The arrest of three members of Sinn Féin in Columbia in 2001, under suspicion of training the Revolutionary Armed Forces of Columbia (FARC), had made the Bush administration hostile towards Sinn Féin, and Gerry Adams' resounding condemnation of the war in Iraq in 2003 only made things worse.

In the years that followed, Sinn Féin began to face increasing pressure locally. In December 2004, in the largest bank robbery in UK history, £326 million was stolen from Belfast's Northern Bank – a robbery that, despite a lack of evidence, was immediately attributed to the IRA. No-one was ever arrested. Then in January 2005, Catholic man Robert McCartney was murdered in a brawl in Belfast, allegedly by members of the Provisional IRA. McCartney's sisters led a very public campaign against Sinn Féin and the IRA, and support for the party, particularly in the Short Strand area, began to wane. Sinn Féin needed to take back the initiative, so in July 2005 they played their trump card – decommissioning.

On 28 July 2005, the Provisional IRA released a statement: "All IRA units have been ordered to dump arms." By September 2005, this had been verified by an independent international commission and the way was made clear for renegotiation of the Good Friday Agreement, something the DUP had been wanting since 2003.

Through the resultant Northern Ireland Act 2006, the secretary of state created a non-legislative fixed-term Assembly, consisting of the 108 MLAs who had been elected in the 2003 election. It met for the first time in May 2006, intending to iron out the difficulties preventing devolution from moving ahead. The discussions that took place in this new Assembly informed the renegotiation, which finally went ahead at St Andrews in October 2006. On 13 October, the St Andrews Agreement was signed.

---

**Main features of the St Andrews Agreement**

1. A legally binding Ministerial Code was introduced.
2. The First Minister and deputy First Minister could now determine if an issue should be decided by the whole Executive Committee, rather than just one minister.
3. If the Executive Committee failed to reach consensus on an issue, then, if any three ministers required it, a cross-community vote on the issue could be requested.
4. If at least thirty MLAs were unhappy with a ministerial decision, they could organise a Referral for Executive Review.
5. The largest party should nominate the First Minister and the largest party in the other main community should nominate the deputy First Minister.
6. Ministers should agree to a new Ministerial Pledge of Office supporting the rule of law, police, courts and participation in all institutions.
7. A new committee, the Assembly and Executive Review Committee, was set up to review the functions of the Assembly and Executive.

---

However, although these were the legal terms of the Agreement, and were all designed to improve the actual operation of devolution (for example, by trying to make it impossible for ministers to go on 'solo runs' in the future), the real issues were, as always, not about procedural matters. The main work of St Andrews focused on the stumbling blocks to devolution between 2002 and 2007: policing, prisoners, parades, Irish language, and power sharing itself.

- **Policing:** all parties had to agree to support the new police force – the Police Service of Northern Ireland (PSNI) – and to take up seats on the policing board.
- **Prisoners:** plans were made for the reintegration of prisoners, and although it was not highlighted at the time, it is now apparent that there was also an agreement concerning on-the-runs. Sinn Féin wanted an amnesty for these and, in most cases, it appears that this was granted.
- **Parades:** plans were made for a review of the parades policy, with the hope that the Parades Commission could be disbanded and decisions on parades could be taken by a mediator appointed by the Office of the First and deputy First Minister. However, this never happened and parades continue to be a contentious issue.
- **Irish language:** this was important to Sinn Féin, and plans for an Irish Language Act were laid down, alongside a range of other equality measures and plans for the promotion and development of Ulster Scots.
- **Power sharing:** a range of changes were made to make it easier for all parties to fully commit to the power-sharing Executive. Safeguards were inserted to specifically ease DUP concerns, for example, measures to make ministerial solo runs difficult. Other measures were designed to make sure that ministers would participate fully in all aspects of devolution, including the North South Ministerial Council (NSMC) and the policing board. The then leader of the DUP, Ian Paisley, said the following: "Unionists can have confidence that [their] interests are being advanced and democracy is finally winning the day."

The St Andrews Agreement set a timetable for restoration of devolution, and obliged all of NI's main political parties to sign up to it by 10 November or face the alternative – a form of joint authority in which the British and Irish governments would take control of the region over the heads of the local politicians and people. All sides signed up and new Assembly elections were held in March 2007, which saw the DUP and Sinn Féin gain even more seats. 'Devolution Day' was set for the 8 May. The DUP and Sinn Féin delivered and took their seats with a relatively amicable and humble approach.

The Good Friday Agreement and the St Andrews Agreement together outline the main constitutional provisions for the operation of devolution. The next two Agreements, Hillsborough Castle and Stormont House, do not cover as wide a range of issues and will therefore be addressed much more briefly.

## Hillsborough Castle Agreement, 2010

At St Andrews, it was agreed that policing and justice powers would be devolved to NI, and it was hoped that this would have happened by 2008. The Hillsborough Castle Agreement was the resolution of this issue. Three years of negotiating, as a result of a considerable reluctance on the part of the DUP to see these powers transferred, finally ended in February 2010 when British Prime Minister Gordon Brown and Irish Taoiseach Brian Cowen signed the Agreement with both the DUP and Sinn Féin. The main result of this Agreement was the transfer of policing and justice powers to the NI Executive. This led to the creation of a new Department of Justice initially led by David Ford from the Alliance Party.

The transfer of policing and justice was seen as a major step forward for devolution. Sinn Féin had been keen advocates of the transfer, and had complained about unionist obstruction over the three years leading up to this agreement. The DUP got some concessions on how parades would be dealt with, but these fell short of the total abolition of the Parades Commission, which many of their supporters would have preferred, causing some to complain – most notably Jim Allister of the Traditional Unionist Voice (TUV). It was only after the formulation of this agreement that the DUP were seen as being 100 per cent behind devolution, so it is a much more significant agreement than perhaps its actual content would indicate. However, it also demonstrated the extent to which the smaller parties were being ignored, as they had been left out of the negotiations and both the British and Irish governments seemed to be only interested in the opinions of the DUP and Sinn Féin.

Overall, it was seen as a success as, right up until the last minute, the support of the DUP was not ensured. Fourteen of its members had been resolutely against the transfer of policing and justice powers until they saw the actual agreement, and then they gave it their support.

**Main features of the Hillsborough Castle Agreement**

1.  The transfer of policing and justice powers to NI.

2.  The decommissioning of weapons by the Irish National Liberation army (INLA), the Official IRA and the South East Antrim UDA, which took place on 8 February 2010 just one day before the amnesty of the 9 February 2010. This was an important step in demonstrating that NI was moving forward on a nonviolent path and could be trusted with justice powers.[7]

3.  The Chief Constable was made responsible for directing and controlling the police.

4.  The role of the Justice Minister was defined.

5.  A working group of six people – three DUP and three Sinn Féin – was set up to investigate a new way of dealing with parades. This did not resolve the issue.

6.  A working group was set up to investigate ways that the Executive could be improved.

7.  The First and deputy First Minister were asked to identify all the areas from St Andrews that had not been resolved and to draw up a plan for full implementation.

## The Stormont House Agreement, 2014

This agreement came about because of two main issues: the failure of the Assembly to deal effectively with flags, parades and the past; and the determination of the British government that NI had to enact the welfare reforms brought in by David Cameron's coalition government.

Cameron had threatened to suspend Stormont if the Welfare Reform Bill was not enacted in an attempt to bring NI into line with the austerity reforms in England and Wales. None of the NI parties were keen on this, but Sinn Féin, in particular, had stood firmly against these changes. As a result of the Stormont House talks, the DUP and Sinn Féin were forced to accept the Welfare Reform Bill and the British government's aim to reduce the size of the public sector in NI.

**Main features of the Stormont House Agreement**

1. A reduction of the fines levied against NI for not implementing the Welfare Reform Bill.

2. More powers over corporation tax granted to Stormont (to help the NI economy).

3. A confirmation of public sector redundancies, mainly from the civil service and teaching.

4. NI Executive would receive £500 million from the UK government to promote shared and integrated education.

5. New agencies were to be set up to deal with the past/legacy issues – for example, a new Historical Investigations Unit to look into unsolved murders.

6. A suggestion that the Assembly should have power over parading. However, there is still no replacement for the Parades Commission.

7. A commission was set up to address the issue over the flag-flying dispute.

8. An agreement to reduce the number of MLAs from 108 to 90 by 2021.

9. The number of departments in the Executive to be reduced from 12 to 9.

10. Politicians who did not want to join the power-sharing Executive would be free to set up an official opposition, if they chose.

Hailed as another breakthrough, the truth was that the Stormont House Agreement did not lead to immediate improvements.[8] Within a few months, it became clear that Sinn Féin were not prepared to fulfil the welfare reforms required under this agreement and that the UK government, led by the Conservatives, was not going to let the issue go.

In August 2015, this was overshadowed by the murder of Kevin McGuigan (suspected of being carried out by the IRA), which refocused attention on the extent to which paramilitaries of all colours remained active in NI. Far from leading to a new era in devolved politics, the Stormont House Agreement led to one of the most serious impasses since 2007. In addition, it soon became clear that some of the legacy issues would be moved to Westminster to be addressed and that other policies, such as the structural changes at Stormont, would bring new challenges of their own, not least the claims by the new opposition parties that the DUP and Sinn Féin were deliberately reducing their (the opposition's) time to speak in the Assembly and making it difficult for them to hold the Executive to account.

Following the Stormont House Agreement, the Executive, in conjunction with both the British and Irish governments, released the *Fresh Start* document, which aimed to demonstrate how the Stormont House Agreement could be implemented. This document outlined six areas of interest ,including ending paramilitarism and tackling legacy issues such as parades. It also had specific commitments with regard to welfare provision and statements of financial support from both the British and Irish governments. Elements of the 2005 *A Shared Future* document can also be seen in this new publication – with its commitment to end criminality and to listen to victims – emphasising the Executive's view that the earlier document was still relevant.[9]

These agreements, taken together, provide a picture of what each institution is designed to do, what powers it has and the limitations of those powers; and the most contentious issues since 1998, as indicated by the issues that keep coming up again and again. What cannot be seen from this is how effectively the institutions have actually carried out their roles, and this will be the main focus in the next two chapters.

### Endnotes

1  This number of ministers can be confusing for students as the Hillsborough Castle Agreement led to another ministerial post being created, increasing the number to eleven. Subsequent reforms have seen the number reduced again to eight.

2  Apparent in 2017 when Martin McGuinness resigned as deputy First Minister thereby causing the First Minister to resign as well and a new election to be called.

3  Cochrane, Feargal, *Northern Ireland: The Reluctant Peace* (Yale University Press, 2003), 194

4  In 2005, Donaldson was exposed as having been an informer for British intelligence since the 1980s. He was killed in 2006 in Donegal by the Real IRA.

5   Cochrane, *Northern Ireland* (2003), 233

6   The failure of the IRA to decommission arms fully before going into government was probably the biggest objection, however reform of the RUC and creation of the new PSNI and the early release of prisoners were all aspects of the original Agreement which unionists had real difficulty in accepting and which continued to undermine the operation of devolution for some time to come.

7   For more detail on this see "Northern Ireland decommissioning body stands down", 9 February 2010, *http://news.bbc.co.uk*

8   One of the most promising and significant aspects of this agreement was the detailed approach it took to dealing with legacy issues (a major source of division not only between politicians, but in the wider community due to their emotive nature). In the Stormont House Agreement (SHA) was a suite of measures for dealing with the past, including: plans to establish an Implementation and Reconciliation Group (IRG); an Oral History Archive (OHA); an Independent Commission on Information Retrieval (ICIR); a new Historical Investigations Unit (HIU) to replace the HET; and a commitment to holding legacy inquests and providing better support for victims and survivors.

9   *A Shared Future* is a document written by the NI office in 2005. It addressed the need to end community divisions, sectarianism and segregation and the need to build a new future in NI based on mutual respect and shared values. The advice in this document was taken on board by different parts of the public sector – such as the education sector or the voluntary sector – where there was an attempt to incorporate its recommendations to help heal divisions and work to end sectarianism.

# THE EXECUTIVE COMMITTEE

# The Executive Committee

This chapter will examine a number of key issues in order to provide a fuller picture of how effectively the Executive carries out its role, and the extent to which it is able to dominate the Assembly. It will begin by identifying the functions of the Executive Committee, as indicated by Strand 1 of the Good Friday Agreement, then move on to describe how the Executive is appointed, including how the D'Hondt system is applied. Following this, the role of the Executive Office (formerly OFMdFM) will be examined, and the remainder of the chapter will offer some assessment on how effectively the Executive Committee has carried out its functions as a power-sharing Executive and in terms of policy fulfilment.

## Functions of the Executive Committee

Executive authority for NI lies with the Executive Committee, making it the equivalent of the British cabinet, just as the First Minister and deputy First Minister are jointly the equivalent of the prime minister. Executive power in any governmental system is power that focuses on setting the agenda and coming up with policy initiatives, while taking responsibility for the day-to-day running of the country. The NI Executive Committee is no different to any other Executive branch, apart from the fact that it only has powers over devolved matters and in some cases a limited input on reserved matters.

The Executive Committee meets at Stormont Castle, rather than in the better-known Parliament Buildings

## What does it do?

The main functions of the Executive Committee are:

1. To ensure the smooth running of the areas devolved to NI, which also means keeping NI in line with the rest of the UK, where applicable.
2. To produce and agree on a Programme for Government, which sets out the policy priorities for the duration of a term of office under a range of headings. This should include specific targets and indicate how they will be achieved. It should reflect the coalition nature of the Executive Committee.
3. To agree and produce a budget in line with allowances from the UK (in the form of a block grant) and in relation to planned expenditure, as outlined in the Programme for Government.
4. To agree proposals from ministers for new legislation in their area of responsibility in the form of Executive Bills.

Any assessment of the effectiveness of the Executive Committee should keep in mind these basic functions, along with the overall function of managing NI on a-day-to day basis, and dealing with any crises that may arise.

## Who is on the Executive Committee and how do they get there?

The NI Executive Committee is made up of the First Minister, deputy First Minister, two junior ministers and eight departmental Ministers. The First Minister and deputy First Minister can decide the total number of ministers in the committee, and this is one of the additional powers they have that stresses their superior role in the committee.

Following the St Andrews Agreement, the First Minister and deputy First Minister are chosen by the largest party from each community after an election. As noted in the introduction, this has been criticised for being one of the ways in which the institutions keep the sectarian divide alive. Between 1998 and 2006 the method was more complex, with both posts requiring cross-community support from a majority of MLAs, including a majority of both nationalists and unionists. This method was changed after the St Andrews Agreement, thereby removing the need for a 'joint ticket'. Both the First Minister and the deputy First Minister can appoint another Executive minister to act on their behalf for up to six weeks, should an emergency arise. This has happened four times:

1. Reg Empey acted for David Trimble between 1 July and 6 November 2001.

2.  Arlene Foster acted for Peter Robinson between 11 January and 3 February 2011.
3.  John O'Dowd acted for Martin McGuinness between 20 September and 31 October 2011.
4.  Arlene Foster acted for Peter Robinson in September 2015.

### The D'Hondt method: How the Executive is appointed

Other ministers are appointed using the D'Hondt formula, named after the nineteenth century Belgian lawyer and mathematician who devised it. It is a method used in other consociational democracies and also in the election of MEPs in the UK. The rationale for using D'Hondt is, in many respects, more important than understanding its actual mechanism. It is chosen because it is seen as the fairest way of allocating seats, and is designed to try to make sure that parties receive ministerial seats in as close a correlation to their overall vote as possible. This method is used to allocate both ministerial posts and the chairs of committees.

So, how does it work? Seats or posts are allocated in 'rounds'. In the first round each party's total vote is divided by one, which really means that the formula has no effect in this round. Following the first round, the total number of votes a party has gained is divided by the number of posts gained, plus one. This means that, the more posts you get, the less chance you have of getting another one unless you had a very big vote in the first place. This may not be clear, but this method does help the smaller parties to get the posts they are entitled to, and keeps the allocation of both ministerial posts and committee chairs fair. The best description of this process is still that by Sidney Elliott of Queen's University Belfast, who described the process on *BBC News in Focus*.[1]

This may seem confusing, but the most important thing about D'Hondt is its rationale or aim to create as fair an Executive as possible. It is a way of making sure that the Executive comprises as many parties as possible, each with a role in the power-sharing model. There is no magic formula to apply and, like many mathematical-based systems, it makes much more sense when it is observed than when it is written down.[2]

### LEARNING OPPORTUNITY

Students should make a list of all the current ministers and their parties using the Assembly website as their source. Pictures should be added for as many ministers as possible.

## The role of the Executive Office (formerly the OFMdFM)

There have been allegations that the First Minister and deputy First Minister, rather like the UK prime minister, have too much power over the rest of the Executive Committee. Indeed, hints of this have been seen in some of the powers mentioned already in this chapter – for example, the ability to appoint another minister to act on their behalf, and their agenda setting power, which is a very powerful tool in deciding the direction of the entire Executive Committee. They have additional support not shared by the other ministers, as a result of having two junior ministers and a whole department of civil servants – the Executive Office or, as it was known prior to 2016, the OFMdFM– both of which are purely to help the First Minister and deputy First Minister complete their duties.

The Executive Office provides invaluable support and guidance for the Executive and especially for the heads of the Executive, the First Minister and deputy First Minister. This is rather like the role of the Prime Minister's Office, which helps to increase the power of the prime minister by giving him/her greater access to research and legal advisors. In the same way, the Executive Office can be a help to the two heads of government: it can research policy areas for the First Minister and deputy First Minister; compile statistical reports for use in Assembly debates; help prepare motions; and advise on how to respond to Assembly questions. In all of these functions they help the First Minister and deputy First Minister be better informed and prepared than ordinary MLAs, which will give them the edge in debates and negotiations.

The strength of the First Minister and deputy First Minister does somewhat rely on how well they work together: those with a good working relationship are more likely to be able to get what they want done by the whole Executive. This sort of relationship was witnessed during the Paisley/McGuinness years and has not really been seen in earlier, or indeed, later dyarchies.

In addition to the support and resource advantage enjoyed by the two leaders, is access to some unique powers that may enable them to dominate the Executive Committee, including:

1. Setting the agenda and time of Executive Committee meetings.
2. Deciding the number of ministers and departments.
3. Deciding if referrals for Executive Review are valid and if those issues should result in wider debate.
4. Holding the casting vote in urgent decisions to be made outside normal Executive Committee meetings.
5. Commanding, as the leaders of the two largest parties, a majority of MLAs together, which may aid the passage of their specific legislative programmes.

6.  Taking the lead role in drawing up both the Programme for Government and the relevant budget. This may have implications for other ministers and how they relate to the First Minister and deputy First Minister.
7.  Attracting the focus of the media, which increases their standing (rather like the UK prime minister).
8.  Taking the lead role in overseas negotiations and relations, including trade.

## Limitations of the Executive

In reality, the two leaders rely on all of the other ministers and, given the nature of the power-sharing Executive, it is harder for the First Minister and deputy First Minister to gain anything like the dominance over the Executive Committee that the UK prime minister has over the cabinet.

One of the reasons for this is the fact that the Executive Committee is a mandatory coalition: in other words, it is a coalition by law. This will always make it more difficult for the head of the Executive to gain total dominance, as there are other political parties involved. Secondly, there is no principle of collective responsibility, which works well in the UK system to silence opposition from within cabinet. Again, because of the power sharing and broad nature of the Executive Committee, it is impossible to have collective responsibility, which therefore reduces the power of the heads of the Executive. Thirdly, the First Minister and deputy First Minister do not get to choose who sits on the Executive Committee in the way that the British prime minister can use his/her power of patronage to choose who sits on the cabinet, which also reduces the amount of control held by the First Minister and deputy First Minister. Finally, they cannot remove a minister and, in fact, the structure of the Executive Committee means that ministers have considerable freedom in their own departments and the First Minister and deputy First Minister must recognise this.

## LEARNING OPPORTUNITY

Students should write a response to the following statement: "Assess the view that the First Minister and deputy First Minister dominate the Executive Committee." They should include positive and negative points, as many examples as possible (but no more than one for each point being made), and a clear conclusion. They should try to do this in twenty minutes.

**Welfare Reform**

Although neither the DUP nor Sinn Féin were completely in agreement with the UK government's welfare reform package, the DUP did eventually accept that it had to be implemented, and both parties had agreed to do so in the Stormont House Agreement. Following the agreement, Sinn Féin refused to implement the measures and, as a result, the Fresh Start Agreement removed this from Stormont control and agreed that welfare reform would be passed by the UK parliament for NI.

## Divisions within the Executive

One of the biggest criticisms of the Executive Committee is that the divisions, an inherent part of a mandatory coalition, make it nearly impossible for it to perform as a cohesive unit. There have been clear examples of problems at Executive level in the past. Divisions over the implementation of the Welfare Reform Act nearly caused the whole system to collapse in 2015, and this had just been resolved when the RHI scandal hit in 2017.

Traditionally the divisions are seen as unionist and nationalist, however more recently there have been growing divisions between the two largest parties (DUP and Sinn Féin) on one side, and the smaller parties in the Executive (Alliance Party, SDLP and UUP) on the other. This came to a head following the May 2016 Assembly elections, and saw the SDLP and UUP take the radical step of pulling out of the Executive Committee, forgoing their seats and forming an official opposition within the Assembly. The Alliance Party are also part of this new opposition group, however, as they have fewer than nine seats in the Assembly, they cannot have official opposition status and the corresponding benefits, such as additional speaking rights, which this confers. This move has radically altered the operation of the Executive Committee and it will be interesting to see how the DUP and Sinn Féin deal with the rigours of government, stripped, as they now are, of their other coalition partners.

It is difficult to accurately assess how prominent divisions within the Executive Committee are. Certainly there are times when there are high profile disagreements and difficulties in agreeing policies – for example over the Maze regeneration proposals, the Irish Language Act, the Welfare Reform Act and the handling of the RHI scandal – but, equally, there is a lot of evidence to suggest that, for the most part, the Executive Committee is able to work well together and to produce a target-driven Programme for Government, which they largely try to achieve.

**Maze Regeneration Project**

The Maze Long Kesh Regeneration Project has been a major cause of disagreement between unionists and nationalists since the prison's closure in 2000. Set up in 1975 to house prisoners who had played an active combatant role in the conflict, it was the location of the 1981 hunger strike campaign. It closed following the signing of the Good Friday Agreement and, in 2003, was put under the control of the Executive Committee. Initially it was suggested the site be used to build a sports stadium, but this plan was shelved and in 2009 the First Minister and deputy First Minister announced that it would be used to build a Peace and Conflict Resolution Centre. This saw the beginning of a heated debate, with many unionists objecting to what they saw as plans for an IRA museum. In 2013 the EU funding for the project was withdrawn and, although the site has been used to host the Balmoral Show, its long-term development plans remain unresolved.

## Ministers, solo runs and fiefdoms

One of the things which is confusing for anyone trying to understand the system of government in NI is deciphering the amount of power held by individual ministers. This chapter has already identified the ways in which the First Minister and deputy First Minister dominate the Executive Committee, but a fuller and more balanced view of this complex relationship can be obtained by considering how much power ministers have in their own departments.

It should be stressed that, in this respect, the NI system is quite distinct from that at Westminster. The degree of individual power held by ministers in the NI system has given rise to the view that they operate their departments almost like little 'fiefdoms', meaning they have the authority to largely do what they want. The UK prime minister picks ministers to head up the various departments and it is expected that, while they will have a fair degree of freedom in coming up with initiatives, it is ultimately the prime minister who will decide if the policies they want to implement go ahead or not.

The system in NI is very different. The ministers are appointed through D'Hondt using the number of votes their party secured at an election, and while this may give some power to party leaders in selecting who, from their party, will get these roles, it does not give the First and deputy First Minister a free hand in selecting ministers. In fact, ministers are expected to have a far greater degree of freedom when it comes to policy initiatives in their departments than would be the case in the UK system. It is exactly this freedom which gave rise to a problem with so-called 'solo runs'.

The term 'solo run' refers to the practice of devising a policy and pushing it through against the wishes of the rest of the Executive, the minister's own department, and in some cases with considerable opposition from the Assembly. Solo runs are examples of ministers acting like dictators in their own departmental area, and have been heavily criticised.

The two most memorable ministerial solo runs were both carried out by Sinn Féin ministers – although it is by no means a practice unique to one party – in the important areas of Health and Education. In 2000, Bairbre de Brún relocated maternity services from the Jubilee at Belfast City Hospital to the Royal Victoria Hospital, building a new regional cancer unit on the vacated site. The move was defended as being part of a general efficiency drive, but de Brún was accused of moving maternity services to her own constituency in west Belfast in order to maintain support there. Then, in 2007, Catriona Ruane took the decision to scrap the eleven-plus exam. This had been a long-standing Sinn Féin policy, initiated by Martin McGuiness when he was education minister, however the arbitrary nature of the decision and the fact that there was no clear alternative to the exam put in place gave rise to a lot of criticism.

Although in both cases the ministers involved could be accused of being heavy-handed, and refusing to listen to opposition, it is equally clear that both acted within the parameters set down by the Good Friday Agreement. It was for this reason that the DUP were keen to see mechanisms added at the St Andrews Agreement that would make it harder for ministers to push through policy in this manner. There have been accusations from all sides of the NI political spectrum that the St Andrews Agreement has failed to stop this, and claims that ministers have indulged in solo runs are frequently made. However, it is equally true that, to date, none have caused the outcry of these earlier two cases.

What the issue makes clear is the unique role of the departmental ministers in the devolved Executive. As part of a mandatory coalition, they have considerably more power in their own departments than the departmental ministers in the UK, and as such can be difficult for the First Minister and deputy First Minister to control, particularly when they are from a different party or from a different community.

Collective responsibility, the convention that the government must at least appear united in public, is therefore impossible in the devolved Executive.[3] The First Minister and deputy First Minister do not appoint individual ministers and therefore cannot force them to resign. Likewise, they cannot demand that all ministers stand behind Executive policies and, in fact, one of the most startling aspects of the NI system is the extent to which the various members of the Executive Committee openly criticise each other's policies, and those of the First Minister and deputy First Minister. Partly because of the cultural expectation of a united and loyal cabinet, an expectation which results from the dominance of the Westminster model in our news and political culture, the apparent disunity and willingness to speak out against each other displayed by the Executive Committee seems very unusual. This continues to be one of the ways in which the Executive appears, to the public, to be ineffective in providing mature government, yet it is a direct result of the very different type of constitutional arrangements made for NI, rather than a result of a lack of internal commitment or mature political behaviour.

## INTERIM SUMMARY

**The Executive Committee is the government for Northern Ireland.**
**It consists of the First Minister, deputy First Minister, two junior ministers and eight other ministers.**

**Its job is to:**

1. Set the political agenda for the five years of its mandate.

2. Ensure economic development.

3. Set sensible and relevant targets for growth.

4. Draw up a Programme for Government which addresses all the policies necessary to fulfil its long-term plans.

5. Draw up and pass a corresponding budget, which will provide the necessary funds to enact the policies and is mindful of the allowances from the UK treasury and other monetary factors.

6. Govern effectively in the areas devolved to Northern Ireland under the four agreements.

## The effectiveness of the Executive Committee

In this section, the record of the Executive Committee since 2007 will be explored with the aim of assessing its effectiveness or otherwise. There are a number of factors which need to be considered in order to form a wide ranging and balanced analysis: the ability to produce and deliver effective Programmes for Government and accompanying budgets; the ability to pass relevant and regionally specific legislation; the ability to function as a power-sharing government; the ability to demonstrate leadership and future planning for NI; and finally the ability to command local, nationwide and international recognition and respect. Each of these will be addressed in order to gain a balanced and thorough picture of the performance of the Executive Committee since 2007.

So, how well has the Executive Committee performed? There is no single clear-cut answer to this question because, as with all aspects of the study of politics, things can change very rapidly. On the one hand, there are those who would say that the Executive Committee has performed better since 2008 simply because it has completed two full mandates. Compared to the period of stop-start suspensions which characterised the early part of devolution between 1999 and 2007 this is an improvement. However, this does not take into consideration the protracted periods of political inactivity which have occurred since, the longest and most notable being the collapse of the Executive in 2017.

The Executive was seen as largely successful between 2007 and 2017, from the time of the St Andrew's renegotiation until the resignation of former deputy First Minister, Martin McGuinness. This had been the longest period of continuing self-government since devolution was reinstated in 1998 and there was considerable evidence that the executive was beginning to get beyond early problems and come to terms with the power-sharing mechanisms. The impact of the RHI scandal and the resulting political impasse called that into question and raised fresh questions among the electorate and political commentators alike about the effectiveness of the Executive and even the ability of the power-sharing arrangements to deliver lasting peace.

**Renewable Heat Incentive**

Set up in 2012 by the Department of Enterprise, Trade and Investment (DETI) – led at the time by Arlene Foster – RHI offered financial incentives to those who wanted to install renewable heat systems. In February 2016, following allegations that the system was being abused, the scheme was closed and an investigation began. The NI auditor general said there had been serious problems with the scheme from the start.

DETI had offered to pay out a subsidy based on every kilowatt of heat energy produced by renewable technologies, but the money that would be received per kilowatt was more than the cost of generating that heat, meaning that the more fuel people burned, the more money they could earn.

The scheme is estimated to have cost £1 billion, with £600 million coming from the Treasury and £400 million coming from NI's block grant. The political fallout from this was considerable, and it ultimately led to the resignation of deputy First Minister Martin McGuinness, which in itself caused the executive to collapse.

This is also referred to as the Cash for Ash scandal.

## The ability to produce and deliver effective Programmes for Government and accompanying budgets.

The first full mandate between 2007–11 saw some progress, and its Programme for Government looked at the following:

- Supporting economic growth – this was a key priority with detailed specific policy areas, such as increasing the number of tourists from 1.98 million to 2.5 million by 2011.
- Promoting tolerance, inclusion, health and wellbeing – including popular measures such as the extension of concessionary fees to provide free public transport to the over sixties.
- Addressing
- Gender inequality – including a commitment to reducing the gender pay gap; eradicating all forms of violence against women; encouraging more women to get involved in politics; and providing access to affordable childcare.
- Reducing deaths from suicide.
- Improving hospital waiting times.

- Encouraging participation in sports.
- Promoting and enhancing the environment – namely reducing greenhouse gas emissions by 25 per cent by 2025; halting the loss of indigenous species and habitats by 2016; and delivering a new sewer project for central Belfast by 2010.
- Investing in infrastructure – with a proposal to invest around £6 billion over the following three years and £20 billion over the following ten years, in order to modernise the entire NI infrastructure. For example, £612 million was to be spent on improving roads and £647 million on upgrading water services (pipes, sewers etc.).
- Establishing an Education and Skills Authority by 2009.
- Reviewing the number of government departments by 2011.[4]

The Programme for Government *Delivery Report*, published on 31 March 2011 and produced by the Economic Policy Unit of the then OFMdFM, states that, by 31 March, the Executive Committee had achieved 67 per cent of the targets set out in the Programme for Government. This overall figure does not reflect how the Executive Committee performed in individual areas, but provides a basis for analysis. It is also important to remember that this is not the only way to measure success and this information needs to be used in conjunction with other factors. The *Delivery Report* outlines what the Executive set as priorities and how well they achieved them, but not necessarily if the priorities they set reflect what the electorate wanted.[5]

In the 2011–15 programme, a number of key priorities stand out, some because they have been accomplished and others because they remain unresolved or are controversial. They include the following aims:

- To introduce a plastic bag levy by 2013.
- To see control of corporation tax devolved to NI.
- To set up a new Education and Skills Authority (ESA) by 2013.
- To develop sports stadia with the IFA, GAA and IRFU.
- To reduce the number of local councils (twenty-six) by creating super councils.
- To develop the Maze/Long Kesh as a regeneration site of regional significance.
- To construct a new Police, Prison and Fire Training College and reform the prison service.
- To promote shared education and to invest £7.8 million in tackling obesity.

This is only a selection of the points from an extensive sixty-page detailed policy document, but it gives an idea of the type of priorities being set and the degree to which they have been accomplished.

A quick look at this selection will illustrate that a number of the issues have clearly been met, for example, NI's council districts have now been amalgamated into eleven super councils, and a plastic bag charge has now been rolled out across the UK, with NI leading the way in being the first to introduce this. In the meantime, control over corporation tax and reforms of the prison service are all underway, while other issues remain outstanding, with the Education and Skills Authority looking, at one stage, as though it was going to be dropped, before it was finally resurrected and rushed through in 2015.[6]

Overall this mandate is judged to be more successful than the previous one with an average success rate of 81 per cent, including preventing the proposed extension of water charges and increase of student fees, both of which are popular policies and well-supported across the community. Therefore, in terms of meeting the criteria of producing Programmes for Government, and achieving their targets, the Executives of 2008–15 have done reasonably well. Likewise, each of these has been accompanied by relevant budgets, although not without some disagreement and disruption. In fact, the 2015 budget saw some serious disagreements in the Executive Committee, primarily over welfare reform. Arlene Foster presented what was deemed by the press as a 'fantasy' budget in June 2015, based on the idea that the welfare reforms were going to go ahead – something that Sinn Féin strongly resisted. In the end the issue was partly resolved but it is a good example of how difficult it can be for the parties to reach agreement even on these less contentious issues.

Regarding setting targets and bringing in policies to achieve them, it could be argued that the Executive Committee has performed its role comparably well, especially when the normal limitations to achieving targets – such as the change in the economic climate or the decline in the block grant from the UK – are taken into account.[7] The general feeling amongst political commentators was that the 2011–16 mandate restored public confidence in the institutions and the Executive Committee. However problems in other areas would soon emerge, undermining this confidence and causing the whole system to be called into question yet again.

In January 2017 the then deputy First Minister, Martin McGuinness resigned in response to ongoing disagreement between the two governing parties on the handling of the RHI issue. His resignation resulted in the fall of the Executive, something that Professor Rick Wilford called a "sharp reminder of the co-dependence inherent in the GFA".[8] In other words the Executive could only exist with the support of all partners, and if one party left it would inevitably fall.

An Assembly election was held on 2 March amidst a bitter campaign, with divisions on Brexit, RHI and LGBT rights playing a key role. This election was also significant in that it was the first since the reduction in MLA seats (from the original 108 to 90) and, generally speaking, smaller parties tend to lose out when a seat reduction occurs in PR-STV systems. The DUP dropped its share of the vote by 1 per cent and lost 10 seats; the UUP increased its share of the vote by 0.3 per cent but lost 6 seats; Sinn Féin increased their vote by 3.9 per cent and lost 1 seat; the SDLP vote share went up by 0.1 per cent and they held 12 seats; and the Alliance Party increased their vote by 2.1 per cent and held the 8 seats they already had.

## Same Sex Marriage Bill

Same-sex marriage legislation was first proposed in NI in 2011 by the Green Party's Steven Agnew and, since then, the issue has been embraced by Sinn Féin as part of their general equality and rights portfolio. The bill has been a cause of division between the DUP and Sinn Féin and is one of a number of new, non-traditional policy differences between the two. In fact, in November 2017, Sinn Féin Leader Michelle O'Neill claimed that one of the reasons for the collapse of power-sharing talks was the refusal of the DUP to support this bill.

It has been voted on five times in the Assembly, and in November 2015 the motion was passed by the Assembly but stopped from coming into law as a result of the DUP using a Petition of Concern. This is an issue which divides voters in NI along age lines with younger voters being much more likely to support the measure than older voters.

The UK and Republic of Ireland legalised same-sex marriage in 2014 and 2015 respectively.

This election was quickly followed by a surprise general election, which confirmed the dominance of the DUP and Sinn Féin. It further strengthened the position of the DUP as they went into a confidence and supply agreement with the Conservative Party to allow Theresa May to form a new government.

Following these two elections, talks between the two main parties in NI failed to result in any agreement and there were calls from MLAs from the smaller parties, such as the Green Party's Steven Agnew, for a reduction in MLA salaries if a new Executive was not formed. The main sticking points were often unclear to the electorate, although it was evident that the enactment of an Irish Language Act, the same-sex marriage proposal, the role of Arlene Foster in the RHI crisis and the difficulty surrounding legacy issues were all part of these discussions.

In November 2017, Secretary of State for Northern Ireland James Brokenshire announced that the UK government would be setting a budget for NI to prevent essential services from collapsing due to a lack of finance. This was taken as an indication that direct rule would inevitably follow, however the UK government made it clear in previous statements that Westminster had no appetite for direct rule, and the preferred option was for a new NI Executive to be formed as quickly as possible. Joint authority had been ruled out by the UK government, although some form of joint stewardship akin to that used in 2006 would be likely if the impasse was to continue indefinitely.

At the time of writing, although talks between the two main parties have broken down again, neither party leader has given up which suggests there may be some progress behind the scenes.

### Irish Language Act

This has been a divisive issue since it was first proposed in 2003. It was promised as part of the St Andrews Agreement in 2006 and re-emerged as a key issue during the political impasse in 2017. Unionists oppose the act on the grounds that it is unnecessary and costly to implement. Nationalists, on the other hand, claim unionists have already agreed to this in the St Andrews Agreement and point to similar acts in both Scotland and Wales, which have not proven to be prohibitively expensive to implement. The association with language and identity has made this a much more divisive issue than in either Scotland or Wales. The debate is more about which culture gets to be seen as the dominant culture in NI than about language. It remains unresolved and divisive.

## The ability to pass relevant and regionally specific legislation

### How does the Executive determine legislation?

The Executive Committee will draw up a Programme for Government and, from that, produce a list of relevant legislation. Like the UK government, it will then timetable the legislation in the Assembly timetable. The relevant minister will present the bill, which will go through several debates and voting stages (see page 94). Ultimately the minister will steer the bill through these various stages in the Assembly in the hope that it will pass easily.

Unlike the UK system, however, there is more cooperation between the minister and the relevant statutory committee and, given the power-sharing nature of the Executive, it is unlikely that an Executive Bill will fail.

### Different Types of Bills

The majority of bills are introduced by a minister from the Executive Committee – these are called **Executive Bills**.

Individual MLAs can introduce bills – these are called **Private Members' Bills**.

Any member of a statutory committee can introduce a bill on behalf of the committee – these are called **Committee Bills**.

As legislative power lies primarily with the Assembly as a whole, the full assessment of legislation will be dealt with in the next chapter. However the majority of successful bills are Executive Bills so it is appropriate to offer some assessment of legislative output as part of its performance assessment.

In legislative terms, 67 acts were passed between 2011–16: 60 were Executive Bills; 5 were Private Members' Bills and 2 Committee Bills. Prior to this, 63 acts were passed between 2007–11: 60 of these were Executive Bills.

Some of the Executive Bills have been extremely beneficial, such as free prescriptions for all NI citizens and free transport for the over-sixties. Meanwhile, the relevant budget acts, usually go through with very little resistance, and the lack of opposition to these is generally seen as another sign of the overall commitment, within the Executive and the wider Assembly, to creating a good solid government.

On the other hand, there have been criticisms of the amount of parity legislation passed – legislation designed to keep us in line with the rest of the UK – and of the Executive's seeming reluctance to pass NI-specific legislation. Though there is evidence to suggest that, as the Executive has grown in confidence, the levels of local legislation are increasing. For instance, examples of Executive Bills from the 2011–16 mandate include: Addressing Bullying in Schools Bill 2015; Shared Education Bill 2015; Rural Needs Bill 2015; Marine Act 2013; and Work and Families Act 2015.

Equally, there are allegations that it does not produce enough legislation overall, as seen when compared to Scotland or Wales (see page 97 for more detail). There have been criticisms that the nature of the power-sharing Executive makes it difficult to produce a coherent overarching set of policies, as it predisposes parties and individual ministers to be more concerned with their own areas, and to fight for resources and legislation in those, rather than thinking as an Executive as a whole.

Both the UUP and the SDLP complained that the lack of an official opposition in the NI government meant that Sinn Féin and the DUP, the biggest parties in the Assembly and the Executive, get their own way on nearly every issue, meaning only policies with the support of the biggest parties will pass. Criticisms can also be made of the way legislation is scrutinised, with statutory committees lacking time and expertise to carry out this role as thoroughly as they would like. There is a serious concern that the biggest parties have overused the Petition of Concern device, enabling them, in an unhealthy and undemocratic manner, to have too much control over legislative output. There have also been criticisms that important issues have been avoided and that the Executive Committee has failed in its legislative duty by not introducing necessary legislation to deal with, for example, legacy issues.

### Dealing with the Past: Legacy Issues

Legacy issues are amongst the most sensitive of the entire peace process, which makes them difficult to deal with, but also essential for the political process to progress. All of the main parties agree that the legacy and impact of the conflict needs to be addressed and all also agree that victims need to be at the centre of that process. However there is disagreement over the definition of a victim, with unionists opposed to using the term 'victim' for anyone who committed, or was involved in committing, acts of violence. Nationalists also have concerns about alleged collusion between state forces and loyalist paramilitaries, and about any talk of an amnesty for soldiers. The St Andrew's Agreement began the process of addressing this difficult area by setting up a Commission for Victims and Survivors, and introducing the Historical Enquiries Team to investigate the 3,269 fatalities from the conflict which have never had a conviction. The HET proved unable to cope with the workload, and was also discredited and viewed with suspicion by both unionists and nationalists for differing reasons.

More recently, progress was made with the Stormont House Agreement, which planned for a range of legacy institutions to be established to deal with this area, including: an Oral History Archive (OHA); a new Historical Investigations Unit (HIU) to replace the HET; an Implementation and Reconciliation Group (IRG); and an Independent Commission on Information Retrieval (ICIR).

To date, although the legislation for many of these provisions has been written and is ready to be presented, they have been held up by political wrangling. The majority of objections have come from the DUP who, in spite of having a public commitment to victims and survivors, have been unwilling to bring the measures deemed necessary forward. The public consultation on dealing with the past was an attempt by the British government to move the process along. Legacy issues continue to be a stumbling block.

Overall the Executive Committee has spearheaded a range of legislation designed to fulfil targets set in the relevant Programme for Government, and the main criticism is not that they have not done enough but rather they have avoided contentious areas, and that the two biggest parties use their numerical advantage to dominate the legislative system.

More importantly, however, is the fact that legislation for NI is now made locally: made for the people of NI *by* the people of NI. Bills are fully debated, amended and subjected to more scrutiny than Orders in Council (the system used under direct rule and its associated 'democratic deficit'). It is also now easier for the general public to get involved, since most legislation goes out to public consultation, and written submissions are considered by the relevant committee as part of the scrutiny role.

### The ability to function as a power-sharing government

On the one hand, there have been no suspensions since 2007 and two full terms have been completed. There may have been times when the institutions were stalled – in October 2015 and again in 2017 [9] – but there was also a desire to keep Stormont going, to find a way to maintain peace and to save the devolved institutions. The institutions developed under the Good Friday Agreement require a mandatory coalition and this was always an uneasy compromise, especially for some unionists who saw it as an unnecessary and un-British way to govern.

The structure of government has allowed for a long period of peace and stability, with the use of D'Hondt to appoint ministers meaning that all parts of the community are represented at executive level. Prior to 2016, all of the main five parties were part of the Executive Committee, which presented challenges but also meant that all of the parties were involved in executive decisions. The fact that unionists and nationalists have been working together on solving problems for all of NI is very positive. It is easy to forget just how much progress has been made given that in the 1980s and early 1990s the DUP would not have considered sitting in the same room as a member of Sinn Féin much less working together on tricky political problems. The good relationship that Martin McGuinness and Ian Paisley formed – earning them the nickname 'The Chuckle Brothers' – was a significant breakthrough and demonstrated political maturity and willingness to work together.

In spite of holding very different views on the constitutional issue, Sinn Féin and the DUP in particular have worked hard to find common ground – for example Sinn Féin giving support to the new PSNI and taking seats on the Policing Board, and likewise the DUP working with the NSMC and fully cooperating on appropriate cross-border schemes. Sinn Féin and the DUP have managed to work together successfully for the vast majority of the time. So much so, that the smaller parties complain about their duopoly and say that they dominate both the Executive and the Assembly.

This arrangement would have been unthinkable twenty years ago. When the Good Friday Agreement was first signed, it looked like the DUP would never accept power sharing, nor sit in the same room as, what they called, 'the Sinn Féin/IRA'. Yet together, these two parties have delivered two full Programmes for Government, along with the budgets to support these, and, as has been seen in the previous section, these have been mainly well-received. The successful negotiation of the Hillsborough Agreement in 2010, which resulted in the transfer of policing and justice powers to NI, was a sign of Westminster's growing faith that the Executive could deliver good government and could be trusted with such a sensitive area. In the later Stormont House Agreement, the Executive again successfully negotiated a reduction in fines for failing to implement the welfare reforms suggested by the UK government.

On the other hand, the failure to act collectively has been much criticised. There was an attempt in the St Andrew's Agreement to ensure closer cooperation between ministers and their departments as a way to improve collective decision-making. Likewise the 2016 Programme for Government was the first to be put together collectively rather than each minister writing their own individual section. Problems remain thanks to a lack of proper collective government – often described as 'sharing power' rather than 'power sharing' – with Cathy Gormley-Heenan using the expression 'power splitting and power snaring' to describe the failure to act collectively at Executive level.[10]

The SDLP and UUP have much criticised the dominance of the DUP and Sinn Féin, whom they saw as taking most key decisions by means of their numerical strength. This has led them to conclude that what exists in the NI Executive is not a true coalition, mandatory or otherwise, but a DUP/Sinn Féin dyarchy, resulting in their decision to form an official opposition, following the 2016 Assembly Elections.

Furthermore, there is evidence to suggest that, within the Executive, ministers remain loyal to their party, and this is further reflected in the Assembly as a whole, with Sinn Féin ministers getting a hard time from unionists and vice versa. In other words, mandatory coalition and the old tendency towards tribal politics remains.

Divisions still exist and have a direct political impact – for example the failure to deal with legacy issues effectively, which led to Westminster having to take direct control of some aspects of this. The argument over funding for Irish Language initiatives and the ongoing debate about the possibility of bringing in an Irish Language Act also shows that significant divisions remain.[11] Likewise the difficulty surrounding the Maze Regeneration Project and the provision of a pension for those severely disabled as a result of the conflict.

In addition to the traditional unionist/nationalist division, there is also a sideways division between the larger and smaller parties. The smaller parties often feel left out of major decisions, for example the Stormont House Agreement, and on numerous occasions have stated that they find it difficult to get legislation through because it relies so heavily on the support of the larger two parties. An example of this would be SDLP Environment Minister Mark Durkan's 2013 Planning Bill, withdrawn after he claimed that amendments to the bill made by the DUP and Sinn Féin would limit the possibility of planning-based judicial reviews and ran contrary to human rights legislation. The formation of an official opposition and the lack of common ground between the parties has arguably made it difficult for the Executive to come to agree on new emerging issues such as same-sex marriage, education and abortion provision for NI.

**Pension for the Severely Injured**

One of the key provisions in the Stormont House Agreement was a plan to provide a pension for those severely injured as a result of the conflict. It is estimated that 490 people in Northern Ireland are currently living with life-altering and limiting disabilities as a result of a conflict-related incident. Although most of those affected will have received compensation through the Northern Ireland Office at the time of the incident, this is not enough to make up for a lifetime of not being able to work. Further, because of an inability to work, these victims have no work-based pensions to rely on in their older years. The issue has proven to be a major stumbling block as the DUP will only grant this pension if it excludes anyone who was injured as a result of their own activity, i.e. if they were injured while planting a bomb. Currently this would be the case for ten people. Sinn Féin on the other hand refuse to support legislation that does not apply to all victims. The position of the Forum for Victims and Survivors NI is that it would be better for the pension to go to all in order to meet the materials needs of those who need it.

## The ability to demonstrate leadership and public service

While the institutions were designed to create a peaceful solution to a long-standing and difficult political situation, these alone cannot deliver peace. Their effectiveness relies on the political will of those elected to hold office.

The Executive has a significant role as it occupies the prime position both locally and nationally and, as such, should lead the way. Effective cooperation amongst politicians working on the Executive Committee can demonstrate to the wider community that collaboration and compromise is not only possible but beneficial. Equally, being able to make positive decisions that benefit all of the community is likely to increase support for the institutions. In this area, and in spite of many challenges, the Executive Committee has demonstrated considerable leadership in a number of ways, may of which go unrecognised.

The 2007–11 era was marked by a business-like approach, which was productive in spite of some problems with gridlock and disagreements. A focus on attracting inward investment, with an emphasis on the creative industries, saw the successful and long-running *Game of Thrones* being filmed in NI with a corresponding boost to the economy. Other films and television productions followed (once word got round the industry that NI had great scenery, cheap accomodation, good links to the rest of Europe and willing extras). The Executive also supported a successful project called Northern Ireland Screen – funded by the Department for the Economy, the

Department for Communities and Invest NI – which plays a role in making sure that there are opportunities to fully develop screen industries as a key part of the NI economy.

The next mandate, 2011–16, had a higher success rate again, with world-class sporting events, such as the Giro d'Italia and the World Police and Fire Games, brought to NI, and with the British Open scheduled for 2019. This Executive also dealt effectively with a number of scandals that could have derailed the institutions – the 2012 flag protests; IRA links to the murder of Kevin McGuigan; and the 2014 on-the-runs scandal.[12] Swirling in the background, meanwhile, were allegations of corruption, and uncomfortable financial controversy with Sinn Féin's use of bogus research company, RSI, and the DUP's alleged financial impropriety in the Red Sky, NAMA and RHI scandals.

### On-the-runs

In 2014 it was revealed that Tony Blair's government had offered a secret deal giving on-the-runs – republicans suspected of, but never charged for, terrorist crimes – immunity via letters which freed them from prosecution. Initially there had been plans to pass legislation to allow on-the-runs to escape prosecution, however objections from unionists and from the SDLP had led to this being shelved. The scheme was revealed in February 2014 at the Hyde Park bomb trial when the accused, John Downey, revealed he had been exempted from prosecution and had such a letter to prove it. The trial collapsed as a result. It was estimated that 187 IRA members, wanted in either Great Britain or NI, were affected. The political fallout was considerable, as old differences between unionists and nationalists were reopened. The situation was eventually resolved and a Westminster Report investigating the scheme was published.

In spite of all of this there is evidence that, in terms of actually setting targets to try to secure economic growth for NI, much was being done. One of the problems was getting this across to the public, and the innovative use of social media via Twitter (#ExecutiveDelivery) was the first of planned measures to try to improve the public image of both the Assembly and the Executive, and to ensure people actually knew what they had achieved.

**RSI, Red Sky and NAMA – allegations of financial corruption**

*Research Services Ireland (RSI):* A 2014 BBC Spotlight programme on MLA expenses found that Sinn Féin had claimed £700,000 in expenses for research supposedly carried out by RSI. However the programme could find no evidence of any research having been carried out and concluded that RSI was a bogus company run by the party's finance managers.

*Red Sky:* Technically this story broke following a 2010 *Spotlight* programme, however it is frequently cited alongside the NAMA and RHI scandals as they are similar and, for the most part, involve the DUP. Red Sky was a controversy which claimed that the allocation of maintenance contracts for the Northern Ireland Housing Executive had failed to follow due process and that contractors Red Sky had had their contract renewed as a direct result of intervention from Nelson McCausland, the then minister for social development. Further, it was shown that Red Sky's work had been less than satisfactory, which raised further questions about why they had their contract renewed. An investigation into the matter in April 2011 concluded that there were concerns about fraud and the contract with the Housing Executive was cancelled at that stage.

*National Assets Management Agency (NAMA):* This scandal saw Peter Robinson accused of personally benefiting from a £1.2 billion property deal. In 2015, Mick Wallace TD alleged that £7.5 million had been lodged with a Belfast law firm to pay off a leading politician after the NAMA deal. The inquiry that followed was equally controversial, with numerous other leading public and political figures criticised at various points. For example, loyalist blogger Jamie Bryson gave evidence to the Finance Committee, claiming that Peter Robinson (and four others) were each to receive a share of the £7.5 million, but Sinn Féin's Daithí McKay (chairman of the finance committee) was alleged to have coached Bryson before he gave evidence, leading McKay to resign his MLA post. Ultimately the scandal was to widen and lead to questions about the way NAMA conducted its affairs both North and South of the border.

## The ability to command local, national and international respect

The transfer of policing and justice powers to the Executive demonstrated a level of political trust from Westminster and a belief in local politicians to behave with propriety and balance. Ministers have been acknowledged worldwide and lauded for their ability to work together.

This was reflected by the attendance of Bill Clinton and other senior world political figures at the funeral of Martin McGuinness in 2017. Indeed in his speech, Clinton openly recognised the progress that had been made and the benefit of continuing peace. In addition, visiting envoys, such as the Iraqi delegation who visited in 2009, have noted how impressed they were by the ability of former enemies to work together to provide government.[13] Overall the successful move from conflict to peace and ongoing attempt to provide solid government is recognised worldwide particularly amongst other conflict-to-peace sites such as Columbia and South Africa.

On the other hand, there have been occasions when the political intelligence and ability of ministers has been queried, for example in the immediate aftermath of the 2017 Assembly election. There is also a real difference between how the Executive is viewed internationally and how it is viewed nationally and locally. For example, a national spotlight has been placed on the DUP following the arrangement to support Theresa May's government, and much of this has been negative in spite of the undoubted increase in political power for an NI party.

Local commentators are also less gratuitous in their praise and more likely to highlight the failings of the Executive than to support them. Arguably the local view is the more important one in the long run since the Executive and institutions rely on the support of the electorate if they are to continue to work. This is therefore an area were the Executive scores better internationally than locally and this might be a problem if it is not resolved sooner rather than later. Continual institutional collapses and an apparent periodic inability to form an Executive due to scandals undermines public faith in the institutions and as such is very destabilising for the entire political system.

Ultimately, any conclusions about how effective the Executive Committee has been may depend on what is meant by 'effective', and what the political environment and circumstances are at the time. The impact of the economic climate or a sudden crisis, such as the 2013 flag protests, cannot be underestimated. Criticisms concentrate on allegations of gridlock and constant quarrelling, and there continue to be problems with divisions within the Executive, as evidenced by the 2015 welfare reform controversy or the failure to form an Executive following the RHI scandal.

However, it could be seen as a long road to a peaceful transition, with small steps being taken to overcome the inherent problems in operating a mandatory coalition which lacks ideological or even, at times, cultural bonds. The following table summarises the main arguments for and against the proposition that the Executive Committee has provided effective government for NI since 2007.

## Executive Committee performance since 2007

| Negatives/how it can be seen as ineffective | Positives/how it can be seen as effective |
|---|---|
| • 'Five into one does not go' – difficulty in making a mandatory coalition work, especially one with so many parties.<br><br>• Lack of collective responsibility and common aims.<br><br>• Problems with gridlock, quarrelling and inability to get over traditional divisions.<br><br>• Problems with emerging new divisions, such as the divide between larger parties (Sinn Féin/DUP) and smaller parties (UUP/SDLP).<br><br>• Failure to address difficult issues – no resolution on flags, emblems and parades.<br><br>• Up until 2016, a lack of opposition leading to too much power for, and not enough accountability of, the Executive.<br><br>• Failure to suggest enough home-grown legislation – too much time spent on parity and European legislation. | • Better than direct rule and its corresponding democratic deficit.<br><br>• Better than the period from 1998 to 2007, characterised by suspensions and stop-start devolution.<br><br>• Has provided local legislation, which is popular and reflects regional needs, for example, keeping university fees lower than in the rest of the UK.<br><br>• Has produced and carried out two full Programmes for Government and corresponding budgets with a fair degree of success.<br><br>• Consociational model provides a good basis for government and has gone a long way to making sure that all sides of society feel represented and treated equally.<br><br>• Some evidence of political maturity has been demonstrated by the DUP and Sinn Féin in particular. Their willingness to work together may be long overdue, but it is also helpful in leading the way in breaking down long-standing sectarian divisions. |

## LEARNING OPPORTUNITY

Students should extend the points made in the summary table above. They should aim to turn each point into a paragraph with the emphasis on explaining why these factors have the impact (positive or negative) that has been ascribed to them. Examples for each point should be added, as appropriate. This also works well as a group activity, with different groups doing different aspects of the extension activity.

## Final remarks

One of the key criticisms of the Executive is the claim that it is unable to function effectively because of its internal divisions. It is important to note that, aside from the traditional unionist and nationalist divisions, there are equally important divisions between the smaller parties and larger parties, as represented by the increasing hostility and resentment exhibited by both the UUP and SDLP, and occasionally the Alliance Party towards Sinn Féin and the DUP.

That there are divisions within the Executive Committee is undeniable, and likewise it is clear that these do cause disruption at a governmental level. However, in order to make a full assessment of the extent to which these divisions cause serious problems a closer look at the evidence needs to be taken. The main contention is that too much time is still spent on outdated issues which reflect a sectarian past, and which fail to deal with the day-to-day issues that affect everyone's lives. This would include issues to do with flags, parades, the Maze regeneration project, the provisions for the Irish language and for Ulster Scots, and lengthy debates about previous agreements and arrangements, such as the on-the-runs agreement that caused such controversy in 2015.

### Parades and Flags

Parades continue to be a contentious issue in NI in spite of the establishment of the Parades Commission in 1998. The majority of parades in NI are organised by the Orange Order, but it has not engaged with the Parades Commission and unionist politicians have called for the body to be scrapped. Sinn Féin have said that marches should only take place in nationalist areas when there has been negotiation between the local residents and those marching. One of the most heavily-disputed parade routes goes past the Ardoyne shops in a nationalist area of north Belfast. This became the centre of a long-standing protest by supporters of the Orange Order, the Twaddell Avenue protest, estimated to have cost £20 million in policing. This protest was successfully ended in September 2016 and agreement between the local Orange lodges and the residents group was made.

Like parades, flags have proven to be deeply contentious. As symbols of national identity they are valued as expressions of loyalty and are clearly used to demarcate areas throughout NI. Tensions over flags were raised in 2012 when Belfast City Council voted on a resolution put forward by the Alliance Party to fly the Union flag on eighteen designated days only, bringing it in line with the rest of the UK. This resulted in widespread condemnation from unionist politicians and an ongoing 'flag protest'. The cost of this protest to businesses in Belfast city centre was estimated at £50 million for the first year of the protest. The issue is not fully resolved. In February 2017, the Supreme Court ruled that the PSNI were wrong to allow the protests to go ahead. Later, in the summer of 2017, new flag rows erupted regarding the flying of paramilitary flags in mixed-housing areas of south Belfast. There has been a concerted effort by some community leaders within the loyalist community to bring these protests to an end.

All of these issues can be seen by those who are uninterested in traditional tribal politics as not only time-wasting and divisive, but as holding back the sort of mature political progress that should have been accomplished by now. The fact that these issues come up time and time again is reference to the fact that they are not fully resolved. While some, or indeed all, of these issues may not be of particular concern to most of the population, they do remain a concern for others, and cannot simply be ignored. Talking about these issues can seem like being stuck in the past for some, but arguably the only way to move the situation forward is to keep talking about them until a suitable solution is found. It is the inability to come up with new ways of thinking, or creative and innovative ways to deal with the past, that is more problematic.

Defenders of the Executive Committee would point out that it is, historically speaking, still early days and, that by working together on more mundane budgetary issues and less controversial policies, these old boundaries will wear away. They would point to the enormous differences in how the DUP and Sinn Féin deal with each other, and even though there are still some very unprofessional and sectarian exchanges, there is a greater acceptance of the viability of each other's opinions. This can be evidenced in their ability to form lasting Executives, something those old enough to remember the 1970s and 1980s would not have thought possible.

The issue of the division between the larger two parties and the smaller parties is an interesting one. Any five-party coalition is liable to suffer from such a division and it is not unexpected. However, it is arguably worsened when the smaller parties are completely left out from key talks with the British government. This is a consequence of the pre-eminence of the First and deputy First Ministers, but it has led to a feeling in the Executive Committee, and among the smaller parties in general, that the two extremes are being pandered to and that the moderates are being ignored. This is a view sometimes echoed in the wider electorate and, though undoubtedly an exaggeration, it is a somewhat understandable conclusion and another of the hurdles that a mandatory coalition brings in its wake. The decision of the SDLP, Alliance and the UUP to withdraw from the Executive Committee following the 2016 Assembly elections reflected their belief that they had not been given a fair hearing within the Executive, and could better serve their constituents by being in opposition.

Other issues taint the Executive Committee, such as the extraordinary number of staff at Stormont in general, but within the Executive Office in particular. Jim Allister of the TUV, who referred to himself as "the one-man opposition", highlighted the extent of the problem and has repeatedly tried to have the numbers reduced. There are actually two separate but related problems here. The first is the unusually high numbers of staff in what was then known as the OFMdFM. In an article in the *Belfast Telegraph*, Samuel Morrison (TUV) noted that the OFMdFM had twice as many staff as the prime minister's office – between them, McGuinness and Robinson had 367 civil servants at their disposal, while David Cameron was able to run his office with 184 – and that the cost of running the OFMdFM was the equivalent of two-thirds of the cost of running the White House, approximately £16,500,000.[14]

The other issue against which Jim Allister spearheaded a campaign was related to special advisors (SPADs) – in particular, who they were and why they had been appointed. He was concerned about the waste of public money, given the wage bill for these officials. In July 2013, he saw his first Private Member's Bill on the issue of SPADs get royal assent, and therefore be passed into law (SPAD Act 2013). This act made it illegal for anyone convicted of a serious crime to be a special advisor at Stormont. It was dubbed 'Ann's Law', after Ann Travers, whose sister Mary had been killed by the IRA. One of those convicted of the murder, Mary McArdle, was later appointed as a SPAD for Carál Ní Chuilín. Travers, a committed victim's rights campaigner, led a movement to have the law changed, to prevent those convicted of serious crime from holding such a post. Sinn Féin regarded this as an attack on them, but the bill received substantial support in the Assembly and was subsequently passed, meaning that another Sinn Féin SPAD, Paul Kavanagh, lost his post (McArdle had already moved on to another job before it was passed).

Building on this, Jim Allister introduced another SPAD bill into the Assembly, this time targeting their pay and conditions. Predictably, this bill was opposed by Sinn Féin, but also by the DUP, as it would affect their SPADs as well. There were, at the time of the proposed bill in 2015, nineteen SPADs at a cost claimed to be about £2 million. Eight of these were in the then OFMdFM. To put this into perspective, Slugger O'Toole's blog noted that this is twice as many as Scotland and three times that of Wales.[15] The new bill would have seen the number of SPADs reduced from eight to four in the OFMdFM, and their salary curbed to come into line with that of a Grade 5 civil servant post (Assistant Secretary). By 2016 SPADs were being paid between £58,452 and £91,809. The proposed change would still allow for a generous salary of between £63,994 and £78,275. In spite of this, there was ferocious opposition from both the DUP and Sinn Féin, who, on 13 October 2015, voted against the bill 52–33. Both the SDLP and the UUP supported the change. The bill failed to pass the second stage and was therefore stopped in October 2015.

These additional issues must form part of our understanding of the operation of government in NI. Not only are they key political issues but they are also valid ways of assessing if the Executive Committee can be said to be properly governing for the good of all citizens in NI. It is unpalatable for those in the public sector, or those affected by ongoing pay freezes, to hear that SPADs are receiving such high salaries, and the situation raises issues about the extent to which they provide good value for money.

At the end of this chapter on the Executive Committee, the important questions to remember are: who is in it, what do they do and how well do they do it? If these three questions can be answered, then it is clear that a good understanding of this aspect of the devolved institutions has been gained. In the next chapter, the role of the Assembly will be investigated and an understanding of how the two institutions work together highlighted.

### Endnotes

1   See www.bbc.co.uk/1/hi/northern_ireland/91150.stm, Sunday 28 November 1999. This is a highly recommended source of additional information for students.

2   One criticism of the use of D'Hondt in the Assembly is that it gives the larger parties more power as the principle is used in selecting committee posts and in choosing who gets to speak in debates. This means that independents and smaller parties find it difficult to get enough time to have their viewpoint listened to and often have to make do with seats on committees that other MLAs do not want.

3   There have been numerous attempts to try to make the Executive more collective in its decision making, and in 2014 Peter Robinson publicly stated that he would personally prefer more collective responsibility and collaboration within the Executive. The 2016 Programme for Government was the first to be collectively constructed and centralised, as opposed to individual departments submitting their 'wish list' and the whole lot cobbled together.

4   For a detailed breakdown see the full Programme for Government available online at www.northernireland.gov.uk/publications/programme-government-2011-2015

5   Programme for Government delivery reports are available on the Assembly website at www.archive.assembly.gov.uk

6   The Maze regeneration remains contentious and therefore unresolved; shared education has become standard practice; the new training college is still under discussion due to a withdrawal of funding from the UK treasury; control of corporation tax was due to be transferred to NI in April 2017 but, due to the political impasse at that time, there was a temporary hold on this.

7   Northern Ireland is largely financed by the UK, with 93 per cent of the entire NI budget being financed by the UK Treasury via a block grant. Any reduction in this grant due to a change in policy at Westminster will have a direct impact on how much money the NI Executive has to spend and can result in planned policies having to be shelved.

8   Wilford, Rick, 'The Northern Ireland Political Landscape'. Paper presented at the Education Service Government and Politics conference, 3 October 2017, Stormont Parliament Buildings

9   In 2015, allegations that the IRA were involved in the murder of Kevin McGuigan led to calls to remove Sinn Féin from the Executive. Chief Constable George Hamilton stated that he believed the IRA were still in existence but not on a 'war footing' and, in September, three leading republicans (including Sinn Féin northern chair, Bobby Storey) were arrested in relation to the murder. First Minister/DUP leader Peter Robinson, along with several of his ministerial colleagues, left the Executive after the DUP failed to get enough support to adjourn the Assembly, and Arlene Foster took over as temporary First Minister. The party then implemented a 'renominate and resign' policy to prevent other parties from assuming the vacated posts. The crisis was resolved when an independent panel was set up to review paramilitary structures.

10  Gormley-Heenan, Cathy, 'Power Sharing in Northern Ireland', *Developments in British Politics 9* (2011, Palgrave Macmillan) pp.130–51

11  Communities Minister Paul Givan (DUP) cut the Líofa budget for the promotion of the Irish language by £50,000, in what was largely seen as a party political move. This decision had to be reversed as it had not been made following correct protocols (Givan claimed the money had been found). Sinn Féin supporters believed it was a petty attack reflecting an antipathy on the part of the DUP to all things Irish.

12  In 2014 it was revealed that Tony Blair's government had offered a secret deal giving on-the-run republicans immunity via letters that freed them from prosecution.

13  This visit focused on power sharing, police reform and the constitutional status of NI. These areas were chosen for their direct relevance to the Iraqi delegation from Kirkuk. The trip was deemed to be a great success.

14 Morrison, Samuel. 'Do Peter Robinson and Martin McGuinness need an office with twice as many staff as Prime Minister David Cameron?', *Belfast Telegraph*, 13 November 2014

15  McCann, David, 'DUP and Sinn Fein vote down Jim Allister's SPAD bill', *Slugger O'Toole*, 13 October 2015, sluggerotoole.com

# THE NORTHERN IRELAND ASSEMBLY

# The Northern Ireland Assembly

This chapter explores how the legislative part of the devolved institutions – the Assembly – works. Following a brief description of the role and purpose of the speaker, the main functions of the Assembly will be identified, and an assessment made of how effectively it carries out its roles. Throughout this process the emphasis will be on the formal powers of the Assembly and how these powers have been utilised in everyday politics. Particular attention will be drawn, where appropriate, to controversial events or to powers which seem to have been abused, as these are areas which cause some public concern about how effectively the Assembly works. The chapter has a detailed analysis of how effective the Assembly is at both legislating and scrutinising the Executive, arguably its two main functions. It ends with an account of how MLAs carry out their roles including their representative function.

The Assembly was first elected on 25 June 1998 under the terms of the NI (Elections) Act. It was called the New NI Assembly in order to distinguish it from the previous power-sharing parliament (established as result of the Sunningdale Agreement in 1973). It met for the first time on 1 July 1998 in

The Assembly meeting in plenary

Castle Buildings on the Stormont Estate, as the Assembly chamber in the main Stormont building was being refurbished and was not ready to be used. Building work was finished in September 1998 and the Assembly has met there ever since. The Assembly is unicameral and therefore requires only one meeting place.

## The Speaker

At the first meeting of the Assembly, Secretary of State Mo Mowlam appointed Lord Alderdice as Initial Presiding Officer for the Assembly. It was the intention that the Assembly would then elect a presiding officer. However, on devolution day, it was decided that Lord Alderdice should be confirmed in the role. In accordance with Assembly Standing Orders, the presiding officer would be addressed as 'speaker'. The role of the speaker is mainly to oversee proceedings in the Assembly and make sure everything runs as it should, but he/she is also chair of the Business Committee and of the Assembly Commission.

The speaker carries out a number of important functions:

- **Legislative** – The speaker assesses the competence of legislation prior to the first and final stages of the bill. He/she sends a copy of the bill to the Human Rights Commission and, on completion of a bill, send a copy to the secretary of state to request that royal assent be given, thereby confirming the new bill as an act of the NI parliament.

- **Ambassadorial** – The speaker receives VIP visitors from overseas to Parliament Buildings. This includes heads of state and senior politicians. The speaker will also host a range of events to promote a wider understanding of the work of the Assembly as part of this ambassadorial role.

- **Procedural** – This is the main role of the speaker and is similar to that carried out by the speaker of the House of Commons in the UK political system. The speaker keeps order in the Assembly, selects amendments to bills and motions for debate, and selects questions for oral answer. The speaker manages the day-to-day running of the legislative chamber, schedules debates, oversees question time, and manages plenary sessions of the Assembly. The speaker is elected by MLAs at the first session of the Assembly following an election.

Given the wide range of roles for the speaker, the Assembly also elects three deputy speakers to assist with the duties. The details of the current occupants of all of these posts can be found at www.niassembly.gov.uk.

## What does the Assembly do?

The Assembly, like the Executive Committee, draws its powers and role from the Good Friday Agreement, as demonstrated from the following excerpt:

> *This agreement provides for a democratically elected Assembly in NI which is inclusive in its membership, capable of exercising executive and legislative authority, and subject to safeguards to protect the rights and interests of all sides of the community.*[1]

There is no doubt that the Assembly was designed to be the main body when carrying out devolved powers. This is in line with British traditions of parliamentary sovereignty and is reflected in the structure of the agreement, and in the following extract:

> *The Assembly operating where appropriate on a cross-community basis will be the prime source of authority in respect of all devolved responsibilities.*[2]

The Assembly consists of 90 MLAs, 5 elected for each of the 18 Westminster constituencies by means of the PR-STV electoral method.[3] The Assembly and its members have three main roles, in common with other legislative assemblies across the world, as follows:

1. To consider and pass legislation – **the legislative role**
2. To scrutinise the work of the Executive Committee and make sure it is spending public money wisely and acting within the limits of its powers – **the scrutiny role**
3. To represent the people who have elected them – **the representative role**

These three functions are the main work of the Assembly and any consideration of how effective the Assembly has been in carrying out its function needs to take these into account. The Statutory Committees are an essential part of the Assembly and all three of these functions are enhanced and can be carried out through the Statutory Committees.

## Legislation in the NI Assembly

Legislation can be introduced into the Assembly in one of three ways:

- as a **Private Member's Bill** – technically known as a **Non-Executive Bill** – by an individual MLA
- as an **Executive Bill**, by a Minister acting on behalf of the Executive Committee
- as a **Committee Bill**, initiated by any member of a statutory committee

The vast majority of bills originate with the Executive Committee, adding to the claims that it has too much control over legislation. Between 2011–16, for example, a total of 67 bills were passed, 60 of which were Executive Bills.

But while individual MLAs tend not to play a leading role in terms of suggesting legislation, some very important and controversial bills have been suggested and passed as Private Members' Bills. Within that same 2011–16 mandate were 5 successful Private Members' Bills, including: Jim Allister's (TUV) first Special Advisers Bill, given royal assent in July 2013 (see page 80); Steven Agnew's (Green Party) Children's Services Cooperation Bill, passed November 2015; and John McCallister's (independent MLA) Assembly and Executive Reform (Opposition Bill), which received royal assent in March 2016 and was the precursor to the Executive Committee changing shape, as it allowed parties to form an official opposition.

MLAs contribute to legislation in a number of ways, and suggesting bills is only one of them. Arguably their most important contribution to legislation comes in debating, making amendments and finally in voting whether or not to pass legislation. Debates and votes take place in plenary sessions of the Assembly, which are held on Mondays and Tuesdays of the weeks when Stormont is in session. These are televised and can be watched by the public from the public gallery at Stormont itself. Most debates have a mediocre turnout, but more controversial legislation, or bills which have a three-line whip applied by their party leaders, will see a much bigger turn out.

The debate and vote on Jim Allister's second SPAD Bill, which sought to downgrade the pay of SPADs, had a vote of 52 against and 33 in favour, indicating a turnout of 85 MLAs in the chamber for that debate and vote. Similarly, the Marriage (Same Sex Couples) Bill 2013, voted on for the fifth time on 2 November 2015, saw an even bigger turnout, with a vote of 53–52 in favour. (Despite this, equal marriage will not be going ahead just yet, as the DUP used a political device called a Petition of Concern to stop the bill).

MLAs also fulfil their legislative role by revising and scrutinising bills as they go through the committee stage, and it is here that they have more of an impact, as the committees are regarded with respect and their suggestions are generally well received within the Assembly. Furthermore, MLAs can have an impact on legislation by requesting that certain pieces of legislation are designated as key decisions, and therefore require special voting measures to ensure they have cross-community support.

---

**The legislative role of MLAs**

1. They can debate and vote on legislation in full plenary sessions on Mondays and Tuesdays at Stormont.
2. They can revise and scrutinise legislation through the committee system.
3. They can request that certain legislative proposals are designated as key decisions and therefore require cross-community support.
4. They can suggest legislative proposals or Private Members' Bills, technically known as Non-Executive Bills.

---

Before considering how well the Assembly has carried out its legislative role, it is important to have a better understanding of the relationship between key decisions, Petitions of Concern, and cross-community support. This is an increasingly controversial aspect of the operation of government in NI, and the use of Petitions of Concern has come under attack for a variety of reasons.

## Cross-community support

Cross-community support is important in the context of NI due to its troubled past and the controversial history of the 1921–72 Stormont government. The desire to have the widest section of the entire population behind new legislation reflects this and is a way of trying to make sure that everyone feels part of the political system and that no discriminatory legislation is passed. While it is desirable to have cross-community support for every decision made, this is not always practical, so only the more significant decisions, such as such as approval of the budget, absolutely require it. These are designated as 'key decisions', are notified in advance, and require special arrangements in order to pass the vote. One of two methods can be used:

1. **Weighted majority** – This requires that 60 per cent of the total members are present and voting, and that 40 per cent of nationalist and 40 per cent of unionist designations present must vote in favour.
2. **Parallel consent** – This requires that a majority of members are present and voting, with a majority from both of the main communities supporting the bill. This is less rigid and less difficult to achieve than weighted majority, but it is the same basic idea.

As part of the provision for cross-community support, all MLAs have to designate as nationalist, unionist or 'other', on taking their seats in the Assembly, and once they have selected their designation they cannot change it. This is to allow for correct counting on cross-community votes.

The controversy arises when the provision for Petitions of Concern are considered. Initially this was intended as another of the safeguarding measures noted in Chapter 1. Undoubtedly well intentioned, it was a device that allowed MLAs to designate legislative proposals where perhaps the Executive Committee had not done so – it was a way of building in an additional safeguard and of redressing the balance between the Executive Committee and the MLAs. Key decisions are identified in advance by the minister introducing a piece of legislation, or are automatically triggered by certain Assembly procedures, such as selecting the First and deputy First Minister. Building in a mechanism that allowed individual MLAs to select pieces of legislation that should be subject to cross-community voting seemed wise and very democratic. Unfortunately, this is not how its actual operation has worked and today it is one of the most criticised mechanisms at Stormont.

## Petitions of Concern

Both weighted majority and parallel consent make it harder to get legislation passed. Other pieces of legislation not deemed to need cross-community support do need a majority to pass, but they are not subject to rules about how many MLAs need to be present at the vote or how many need to support it from both of the main communities. In other words, if a piece of legislation is considered to be a key decision, or needs to attain cross-community support, it is less likely to pass.

This mechanism was designed to prevent either community feeling dominated by the other, or, to be more precise, to prevent any type of discriminatory legislation from being passed. Petitions of Concern are an important power for MLAs and they are a legislative tool that MPs do not have. A Petition of Concern needs the support of at least thirty MLAs in order for a matter to be designated as a key decision and the subsequent voting mechanisms initiated. In the 2011–16 mandate there were 115 Petitions of Concern covering a range of issues: Marriage Equality (used four times); Welfare Reform (used 48 times); and the Education Bill (used 9 times).

An optimistic view of the use of this device is that it has prevented the enactment of unequal legislation, but there is an argument that it has been overused in order to play party politics and, as it takes thirty MLAs to launch a successful Petition of Concern, it undoubtedly favours the bigger parties. After the 2017 Assembly election, for example, the DUP had 28 MLAs and Sinn Féin had 27 MLAs, giving both of these parties an obvious advantage (although not as much as they had prior to 2017).[4] The smaller parties have much less chance of abusing this procedure and they are among those who have claimed that it is being misused. Indeed, there is good cause to suggest that it has become an anti-democratic device by strengthening the already very strong position of the two biggest parties in the Assembly at the expense of the smaller ones.

Recent Petitions of Concern seem to be much less about preventing discriminatory legislation from being passed and more about larger parties being able to see their agenda forced onto the Assembly.[5] Possibly the most controversial to date is the DUP's invocation of a Petition of Concern to prevent the passing of the Marriage (Same Sex Couples) Bill, when in 2015, on the fifth attempt, it finally passed a Stormont vote. The DUP, adamantly opposed to gay marriage, and equating the passage of this bill with an attack on Christianity, immediately launched a Petition of Concern to stop the measure being passed. This caused a spokesperson from Amnesty International to wryly note that a mechanism designed to prevent abuses of power was being used to uphold discriminatory practice.

One of the lesser-known aspects of the Stormont House Agreement was a commitment to reform Petitions of Concern, and the mechanism is currently under review at the Assembly. It remains to be seen, however, if the larger two parties will be keen to reform a device that has proved so useful to them and has, in effect, given them a veto over the legislative proposals they dislike.

### LEARNING OPPORTUNITY

In pairs, students should research the cases for and against Petitions of Concern, referring to actual examples and taking into consideration the purpose of this mechanism. They should then write up and present their findings to the whole class as the basis for a debate on the topic.

## How is legislation passed in the Assembly?

This is often an aspect of the legislative process that students spend too much time learning. At A level and beyond, the real concern is what type of legislation is being passed, who is (and who is not) getting to pass it, and how it can be reviewed or stopped, rather than the actual stage-by-stage process. In other words, students do not need to go through the various stages and, in fact, when this is done, it is often at the expense of other more relevant material.

However, it is important that the process is made clear for a general understanding of how the legislative system works. Some knowledge of this will also be useful in forming preliminary opinions about how democratic the process is, before looking more analytically at legislative performance since 1998. What follows, therefore, is a summary of the stage-by-stage process of passing legislation in the NI Assembly.

**The legislative process in the NI Assembly**

Pre-legislative scrutiny

First stage: title of bill read out

Second stage: debate on bill's general principles

Committee stage

Consideration stage: MLAs vote on Committee findings and submit amendments

Further consideration stage: second opportunity for MLAs to amend bill

Final scrutiny

Final stage: Assembly debates on whether to pass bill

Bill checked by Attorney General and Advocate General for legislative competence

Reconsideration stage: this only happens in exceptional circumstances

Bill receives royal assent and becomes law

Although on paper this appears a lengthy process, and indeed given the various stages, reports, debates, checks and votes it is not surprising that each bill takes some time to become law, there *is* a way of making legislation in a hurry. This is reserved for special cases or for emergencies and involves the use of what is called an Accelerated Passage Procedure. As the name suggests, it allows a bill to go through all of the stages more quickly, bypassing the usually all-important committee stage altogether. By using an accelerated passage procedure, a bill can be passed in just ten days. The minister responsible for the bill must explain why accelerated passage should be used and gain Assembly support before it is utilised. It has been used in the Assembly to pass Budget Bills, for the Pension Regulator Tribunal Bill 2009, and for the Welfare Reform Bill 2007. In all of these cases it was relatively uncontroversial, as it was being used primarily to push through parity legislation. However, the initial decision to use this procedure to pass a Victims' Commissioner Bill and for the Local Council Bill was more controversial.[6] Unlike the Petitions of Concern, this does not seem to be subject to parliamentary abuse but it is certainly a potentially divisive procedure. For the most part, however, it seems to have been used with caution and only to try to get legislation through in a timely manner.

## How does the Assembly perform as a legislative body?

### The criticisms

Having clarified how legislation is passed, and some of the procedures associated with the legislative process, it is now possible to measure the effectiveness of the Assembly as a legislative body. There are a number of criticisms that have been levelled at the Assembly regarding legislation, and each of these will be addressed as fully as possible.

Firstly, is the commonly-held view that, as a legislative body, it has failed to produce enough 'home-grown' legislation. A distinction is drawn here between regional-specific legislation and 'parity' legislation. Although there is nothing wrong with parity legislation per se, if the majority of the legislation passed by the Assembly is parity legislation, then why have an Assembly at all? Why not just let Westminster rule and have done with it? The benefit of having a local parliament is that it can make regional-specific legislation to reflect the needs of the local area, and if it is not doing that, then there really is not any need for it. The only way to assess the validity of this criticism is by examining the bills that have been passed into law, and working out how many of these have been parity bills and how many reflect a more regional slant.

The second criticism is that the Assembly is simply not producing enough legislation, parity or local, to justify its existence. This argument hinges on assessing how many bills would be regarded as 'enough' for a regional assembly, and then comparing the answer to the legislative record for NI since 1999. A comparison with other devolved assemblies (rather than with Westminster) would be the best way forward for this exercise and, as an approximate measure, a comparison to the legislative output of the Scottish parliament will help clarify if the volume of legislation passed at the Stormont Assembly is reasonable.

Finally, like any legislative Assembly, there is an allegation of Executive dominance in legislation. The vast majority of legislation passed originates with the Executive Committee and, although this is partly to be expected given that its job is to introduce legislation required to meet the Programmes for Government, it is also unhealthy if it appears that there are not enough opportunities for individual MLAs to introduce legislation.

### *Too much parity legislation?*

By reading the summary of each bill, and cross-referencing the bills with the legislative record for the UK at the same time, it is possible to get a better idea of how much of the legislation is so-called parity legislation. These figures are, to a degree, approximate because in some cases a bill introduced in another part of the UK may result in the demand for a similar measure elsewhere in the UK, and therefore the corresponding legislation, whilst not NI-specific, does reflect a regional need or desire. An example in reverse is the Carrier Bags Act 2014, introduced in NI and later taken on by other parts of the UK.

With this proviso in place and if Budget Bills are taken out of the equation (since they are not introducing a specific policy and would be needed for both parity and regional legislation), then the total number of regionally-specific bills for the 2011–16 mandate was approximately 42. That is, 42 out of a total of 67, which is 63 per cent. If Budget Bills are included in the calculations and accepted as regionally-specific and necessary legislation, then the figure rises to 52 bills out of a total of 67, which is 77 per cent. It is important to understand that the Budget Bills are the Executive's way of providing the necessary funds to enable policies, which have been approved by the Assembly to be enacted. In the 2011–16 mandate there were 10 Budget Bills in total.

Therefore, if this rough estimate is accepted, even 42 bills out of a total of 67 is a fair record, meaning that the statistics do not really reflect the first criticism, that the Assembly fails to produce enough regionally-specific legislation. Looking at the quality, rather than the quantity, of the bills produced, provides an even better idea of whether the legislative record of the Assembly is sufficient. Measures such as the freeze on university tuition fees in the Student Loans (Amendment) Act 2011, or the decision to keep the Educational Maintenance Allowance (EMA), are popular with students and their parents. Likewise, the provision of free transport to the over sixties and free prescriptions are all welcome legislative developments for the NI electorate, irrespective of community background. Bills such as the Water and Sewerage Services (Amendment) Bill 2013, which was enacted in March 2016, can easily be missed by the general public, as they are unlikely to get much media attention, but they do help make services in NI more effective, and in this sense are an essential part of updating our infrastructure. Very few of the bills are of the traditional tribal nature. In fact, it is hard to find any very obvious bills of this sort by simply looking at the lists of bills passed – except, perhaps, the early bills passed after the restoration of devolution in 2008, for example, the Commission for Victims and Survivors Bill 2008. There is far more legislation aimed at upgrading infrastructure, roads, water supply, and how the judicial system works, as well as improving the way in which devolution itself works. There has been criticism of the speed with which MLAs voted themselves a pay increase in one of their very first pieces of legislation, but overall a fair degree of relevant local legislation has been passed.

### Not enough legislation overall?

What then of the complaint that there simply is not enough legislation to justify the expense of a local devolved assembly? The only way to really assess this is to compare the legislative output of the Assembly with that of the Scottish parliament, and to a lesser degree the National Assembly of Wales.

Between 1999 and the end of 2014, the Scottish parliament passed 218 bills into law. This gives a yearly average of 13.6. For the same time period, the NI Assembly passed a total of 132 bills into law, giving a yearly average of 8.2. However, if the years of suspension in Northern Ireland are factored in, and deducted from the calculation, there is an average of 12 bills passed into law each year, which compares favourably with the Scottish Parliament's record.

The National Assembly of Wales does not have the same level of devolved powers possessed by either Scotland or NI, and it is for this reason that comparisons with Wales can be only very generally made. The Welsh Assembly only gained legislative power for primary legislation after 2007, and its record indicates a yearly average of 6 bills passed into law, though it is only fair to point out that there is a much higher degree of secondary legislation passed, reflecting the unique position of Wales and its deeper ties with the English legal and judicial system.

In conclusion then, it would appear that the second criticism, that there is not enough legislation from the Assembly, is not backed by statistics, and although there is clearly fluctuation across the years, the amount of legislation overall compares favourably with that of the Scottish Parliament.

### The dominance of the Executive?

Finally, is there evidence of Executive or government dominance in legislation? An initial exploration of the Assembly website – where Executive and Non-Executive Bills are clearly labelled – will reveal the following key legislative statistics (accurate at the time of writing):

| Date | Executive Bill | Private Members' Bill | Committee Bill | TOTAL |
|---|---|---|---|---|
| 1999–2011 | 103 | 2 | 0 | 105 |
| 2011–16 | 60 | 5 | 2 | 67 |
| 2016–17 | 1 | 0 | 0 | 1 |
| TOTAL | 164 | 7 | 2 | 173 |

If looking, for example, at the bills passed in 2011–16, and accepting that this is representative of the overall pattern for Executive versus Non-Executive Bills, then it would mean that approximately 10 per cent of bills are Non-Executive in origin. Although this figure is low, it is in keeping with the Westminster parliament.

In addition, it should be noted that there have only been seven Private Members' Bills passed in the NI system, and since five of these have been in the recent session, it may be the case that MLAs are getting better at pushing their legislation through.

The Assembly Bill Office would confirm that there have been relatively few successful private Members' Bills to date, but they anticipate a lot more coming forward for consideration in the future. As Stormont gets through a lot of 'catch up' legislation designed to update NI's infrastructure, there should be more time for constituency and cause-based legislation.

There is also a sense that MLAs are becoming more confident in introducing their own legislation. It is significant that John McCallister, who introduced the first successful Private Member's Bill – the Caravans Act 2011 – went on to successfully steer a second Private Member's Bill through the Assembly. That bill – the Assembly and Executive Reform (Assembly Opposition) Bill 2016 – has arguably altered the very way the Assembly operates, as it was designed to create a collective style government within the Executive, and to allow for an official opposition. There was considerable support for this measure as it passed through the Assembly, and it has brought about a significant constitutional change, adding weight to the view coming from the Assembly support staff that individual MLAs are only now starting to come to terms with their roles and responsibilities, and will only get better and more active in this area in the future.

It must be remembered that there are other ways of measuring success, rather than just focusing on whether or not the bill gets passed. Private Members' Bills help to raise the profile of key issues and widen or introduce debate on important areas, which may lead to a change in the future. In addition, there is evidence to suggest that sometimes an individual member will suggest a bill that is then taken up by the Executive. So while it passes as an Executive Bill, it has actually started life with an individual MLA. This was the case with Daithí McKay's Carrier Bags Bill, which started as a Private Member's Bill and ended up being taken through by the Executive; likewise the extension to NI of the Marriage (Same Sex Couples) Act 2013 was originally proposed by the Green Party's Steven Agnew before being championed by Sinn Féin.

### What role do MLAs play in legislation?

As has been seen, MLAs play a role in the making and passing of legislation in a number of ways. They can suggest legislation in the form of Private Members' (Non-Executive) Bills; they can suggest amendments or revisions to bills during debates in plenary sessions or during the committee stage; and finally they get to vote on the final bill to decide if it will become law or not.

The ability to amend legislation is equally important, and the Assembly education service noted, in a circular to teachers sent in April 2016, that during the 2011–16 mandate a total of 1,953 amendments had been made to bills.

| How successful has the Assembly been as a legislative body? | |
|---|---|
| *Positives* | *Negatives* |
| • The Assembly has completed two full sessions and delivered two Programmes for Government. This is a significant progression from the stop-start period that preceded it. | • Still too much parity legislation and not enough local legislation, although there are two caveats to this. Firstly, there is evidence that it is starting to change; secondly, part of the problem is a lack of awareness of what exactly the Assembly does. |
| • There is evidence that regional-specific and popular legislation is being produced to target local needs. | • Still too much time in debates spent on old traditional tribal politics, particularly those involving the past, flags, emblems and culture, leaving little time to fully address some important issues. |
| • There has been an effort to produce legislation to address the serious problem with infrastructure and updating. | • Some evidence of party dominance and the rise of career politicians who do not vote against their own ministers, both in votes and in committees. Made worse when parties do things like threaten to fine MLAs who vote against the party whip. |
| • Allegations that all legislation is parity legislation and that there is not a high enough volume of legislation do not hold up to statistical analysis. | |
| • Individual MLAs have successfully steered through seven Private Members' Bills and it is believed that this average will increase in the next session. | • Lack of an experienced official opposition, which arguably makes it easier for the Executive to dominate the legislative agenda. There is strong evidence of Executive dominance to support this. |
| • MLAs have carried out their legislative role by voting on, debating and analysing bills in the Statutory Committees. | • Evidence of continuing divide in new emerging issues, such as gay marriage and eleven-plus. |
| • Petitions of Concern, although highly controversial and undoubtedly abused, have been used as a political tool by both MLAs and their respective parties. This indicates that MLAs are using all the political tools at their disposal. | • Petitions of Concern have been considerably abused and if they are not reformed will continue to undermine the work of the Assembly. |

## LEARNING OPPORTUNITY

Using the information provided in this section, together with their own knowledge, students should complete a timed essay addressing the proposition "The NI Assembly is a legislative failure": Discuss.

## Scrutiny in the NI Assembly

The second major function of the Assembly is to scrutinise the Executive Committee or to hold it to account. This is a vital role, as it ensures that the government of NI (Executive Committee) is acting within the law, following the proper processes as laid down by the constitutional arrangements for the devolved institutions, and, in part, trying to make sure that they are spending public money wisely. Often this is an area which students struggle to understand, as it seems less tangible than the passage of legislation. However, an examination of how they carry out this role will clarify both how it is done and why.

The ability to scrutinise government is an essential aspect of democracy, as it ensures that the government is acting properly at all times and not going beyond their powers. Given the historical background and deep communal divide which gave rise to the devolved institutions in the first place, the Assembly's ability to effectively scrutinise the work of the Executive Committee was, in addition to being a core feature of democracy, another way of appeasing underlying fears about any potential inequality in how it would operate.

There are a number of mechanisms designed to help the Assembly carry out its scrutiny role, which include: Statutory Committees, question time, oral and written questions, and adjournment debates. There is a striking similarity here between the scrutiny methods available to MLAs and those available to MPs in the UK Parliament. However, the one difference would be in the committee system, which in NI rather unusually requires committee members not only to work in collaboration with each other and the relevant minister in legislation, but to also be prepared to scrutinise the minister when necessary. This strange and seemingly impossible arrangement has surprisingly worked well and it is in this section that the committee system at Stormont is investigated, while bearing in mind that they are not simply an organ for scrutiny of Executive actions, but also have a vital role in legislative scrutiny.[7]

## Assembly committees

There are four main types of committees in the Assembly:

- **Statutory Committees:** There is a Statutory Committee for each government department and their role is to both assist and scrutinise the minister and the department. They combine the roles of the UK Select and Public Bill Committees into one body.
- **Standing Committees:** These committees are permanent and are set up

to make sure the Assembly runs smoothly. The best known of these is probably the Public Accounts Committee, whose job it is to make sure that all of the accounts for Assembly business are accurate. A second significant standing committee would be the Chairpersons' Liaison Group, which is a committee made up of the chairpersons of all the standing and statutory committees.

- **Ad Hoc Committees:** These are temporary committees set up to deal with a particular issue, so once the investigation or enquiry is complete, the committee is no longer required. An example is the Ad Hoc Committee on Local Postal Services, which presented its findings to the Assembly in 2008. A more recent example would be the 2011 Ad Hoc Committee on the Assembly Members (Independent Financial Review and Standards) Bill.
- **Joint Committees:** These consider matters that affect more than one committee. They are set up as temporary committees when a matter that affects policy in more than one department is under consideration in the Assembly. An example is the 2010 Joint Meeting of the Committee for Justice and Committee for Health, Social Services and Public Safety. This joint committee met on a weekly basis to consider matters that were important to all of the departments involved.

By far the most significant of these for the general day-to-day operation of government are the Statutory Committees. However, it should be remembered that some of the others play important roles in maintaining standards among members (Standing Committee on Standards and Privileges); making sure that the money required for policies is available and being spent wisely (Public Accounts Committee); and promoting better coordination between all the committees (Chairpersons' Liaison Group). The need for reform of Petitions of Concern, would fall under the remit of another Standing Committee – the Assembly and Executive Review Committee. This highlights the fact that it is not only Statutory Committees that deal with topical issues.

It is certainly worth a look at the role and remit of the various Standing Committees by visiting the Assembly website. There you will also find information on what issues have stimulated the creation of Ad hoc (Temporary) Committees – such as the proceeds of crime, and flags and emblems. Understanding the role of the committees, or even just knowing that they are investigating a range of issues, will help inform accurate conclusions about their effectiveness.

The membership of all of the committees is determined by party strength – that is, the largest parties have more members on the committees. Without doubt, this sometimes means that the larger parties have an easier time, especially if they are able to rely on loyal party members being unwilling to challenge ministers from their own party. The committee chairs are picked by the D'Hondt formula and the position must go to an MLA from the opposite designation to the minister: a unionist minister will have a nationalist chair leading the relevant Statutory Committee for their department, and vice versa. By agreement, committees have eleven members – a practice preferred by all in the Assembly. However, this may have to change with the reduction in the number of MLAs, as it is already difficult for ministers to carry out all of their roles, and currently most MLAs will be members of at least three committees. Meetings are held weekly and last for two to three hours.

### Statutory Committees

The Statutory Committees provide the main way of scrutinising the government (Executive Committee) and there is one for each Executive department. They have been given extensive powers, partly in recognition of the possible reduction in Executive scrutiny, which might come from potentially having no official opposition in the Assembly. Though, even with the existence of an official opposition, the Statutory Committees remain the main form of scrutiny of the Executive, so any investigation into their effectiveness should begin by looking at their powers and actions since 2007.

The Statutory Committees have a number of significant powers:

1.  **The ability to scrutinise legislation line by line**, and to suggest relevant amendments. This power implies a conflictual relationship between the committee and minister, though it is more commonly the case that the committee and minister work together to try to produce good quality legislation. The Assembly Education Service estimates that 76 per cent of amendments suggested by the Statutory Committees are accepted, indicating that this is a significant power and is used to good effect.

2.  **The ability to scrutinise the actions of their minister** (and, unlike the UK system, this is difficult to avoid). In order to do this, the committees have the power – reinforced by Section 44 of the Northern Ireland Act 1998 and Standing Order 46(2) – to call for 'persons and papers'. This means that the committees can ask

for witnesses to come before them; oblige ministers to attend hearings and answer awkward questions; and ask for all relevant documentation to be made available for their investigation. These scrutiny powers are taken seriously by the committee members who can, and do, ask some very difficult questions. On the other hand, Professor Rick Wilford of Queen's University claims that they act more like 'party animals' than political animals – that they are still reluctant to criticise their own party when in the committees.[8] Committee reports are available online at www.niassembly.gov.uk for further information, as required.

3. **The ability to conduct inquiries.** Ultimately, committees, if they remain dissatisfied with their minister's responses, or if they have an issue raised by a stakeholder (someone who has a key interest or solid knowledge of that area, for example, the Housing Executive in the case of a social housing matter), or as a result of the press or public interest, can start an inquiry. The inquiry will be held like any other legal inquiry, requiring detailed hearings and lengthy discussion. One of the most high-profile inquiries held by a Statutory Committee in the 2011–16 mandate was that held by the Committee for Social Development. Following a *Spotlight* programme in July 2013, this committee had to suspend most of its other work and investigate claims that Social Development Minister Nelson McCausland, had acted inappropriately in attempting to extend a Housing Executive contract with a maintenance firm – the Red Sky scandal (see page 75). This inquiry revealed the effectiveness of this process, as the committee found against the minister. However, it also said that there were limitations to its powers, and in its summary called for more extensive powers of investigation to be made available.

4. **The ability to suggest change.** Once they have looked into a matter, committees will publish reports which will then go to the Assembly for debate. It is then up to the full Assembly to decide whether the report recommendations are enacted, and if the minister is present he/she is expected to respond. The minister is then expected to give a written response to the committee within two months. According to the Assembly Education Service, approximately 70 per cent of the committees' recommendations are taken on board.

5. **The ability to hold reviews.** Apart from full inquiries, committees can hold reviews that allow them to explore certain issues. An example of this is where the Assembly Education Committee looked into

the matter of potential changes to A levels. These reviews allow the committees to keep up-to-date with issues as they arise, and make them better-informed when dealing with relevant legislation.

### The relationship between ministers and committees

Although this section would suggest that the relationship between the departmental ministers and their relevant committees is a conflictual one, the opposite is in fact closer to the truth. Behind the scenes, the vast majority of the time the minister and his/her committee work together trying to get through as much legislation as possible in their relevant area. The bulk of their time is shaped by Forward Work Plans, which outline the committee's work for each session. These plans are largely constructed in line with the relevant minister's policy proposals and are designed to help see these proposals go through as quickly and efficiently as possible.

There is little time left for inquiries and this may be a potential criticism when it comes to their scrutiny role. Most MLAs are focused on getting the Executive's legislative programme through, and because of time constraints, this can make it difficult for them to be very active in Executive scrutiny. According to Professor Wilford, reforms of the committee system, in line with the reduction in the number of Executive departments, could mean that it will become more difficult for committees to carry out all of their functions.[9] The worry then, is that legislation would take priority, with scrutiny lagging behind, if in the reformed system there were fewer committees, fewer MLAs and just as much work to do. This remains to be seen, but at present it does appear as if there may be an accountability issue with some of the reforms to the structure of the Assembly and Executive.

### Questions for Oral Answer, Written Questions and Adjournment Debates

The Assembly may also hold the Executive to account by questioning ministers (including the First Minister and deputy First Minister) about their areas of responsibility and about issues that concern them or their constituents. This is done in two main ways: Questions for Oral Answer and Written Questions.

The first, Questions for Oral Answer, is done via Question Time in the Assembly.[10] Time is set aside in the Assembly for direct questioning, ministers having submitted their questions in advance. Twenty of these will be selected randomly by a computer programme for the minister to answer, and MLAS will have an opportunity for a follow-up or supplementary question, where they can press the minister for a more detailed response if they feel the issues have not been fully addressed. As these sessions are televised, and the public gallery is open, ministers do not want to be seen to be evasive or ill-informed, and will therefore attempt to answer the questions to the best of their ability. Any questions which are not answered during the session will receive a written answer from the minister. Since September 2013, MLAs have been allowed additional time at these sessions to question ministers, as a result of the introduction of a new scrutiny procedure – Topical Question Time – which gives them 15 extra minutes to question ministers on current issues. Significantly, ministers will not have advance notice of these questions.

MLAs can also submit Written Questions to other ministers, and this is a good way for MLAs to raise very specific issues or issues which relate to a very specific constituency concern. Ministers are expected to reply in a timely and informative manner. There is a limit of five questions per day for each MLA, which does not seem overly restrictive. Some MLAs prefer using written questions, as it is harder to deny a response if it is written down.

Finally, MLAs can raise issues in Adjournment Debates, which are held at the end of plenary sessions, usually on Tuesdays, between 3 and 6 p.m., thus allowing plenty of room for discussion. These debates also provide the opportunity for MLAs to raise constituency concerns, which means they serve as a representation tool as well. This scrutiny method is often overlooked.

### How effective are these methods of scrutiny?
All of these methods give MLAs a range of ways to hold the Executive Committee to account, but none of them are without their downside. Ministers can still ignore their committees, although admittedly not on the scale experienced before the St Andrews Agreement, when many of the infamous solo runs took place. Question time suffers the same limitations as that of the UK system, namely that ministers know the main question in advance. However, as in the UK, ministers can get caught out so they mostly try to explain things as clearly as possible to the Assembly, rather than hide anything.

The lack of a formal opposition was seen as a potential problem and one which has been addressed by John McCallister's Assembly and Executive Reform (Assembly Opposition) Act 2016. In Westminster, one of the accepted roles of the official opposition is to keep the government on its toes, to ask awkward questions and force the government to explain itself. This is seen as good for democracy, and the official opposition, which in the Westminster system is the second biggest party, can access money for research and other forms of assistance in order to fully carry out this role. The lack of a formal official opposition was regarded as limiting the effectiveness of scrutiny in the Assembly, and there is evidence to suggest that Sinn Féin and the DUP do join forces in order to get their agenda pushed through. This has led to smaller parties, referring to the setup as a Sinn Féin/DUP duopoly, and explains why the smaller parties decided to go into opposition together following the 2016 Assembly elections. The first official opposition day was held on 26 September 2016, when questions were asked about NAMA, pensions for women, and rural banking.

## How independent is the Assembly from Executive control?

Everything that is discussed in the sections on legislation and scrutiny has relevance for this key question. Rather like an executive dominance question in the British Politics module, a broad-based question like this will require a consideration of both the extent of legislative and scrutiny power and its limitations. The key difference is the consociational nature of the NI system which requires a power-sharing Executive. This arguably creates a situation whereby the Executive is even less likely to be challenged as there may be as many as five of the main parties on the Executive, making them unlikely to vote against Executive legislation.

However given the unique way the statutory committees work in NI and the tendency for party loyalty to be more important than Executive loyalty this has not been a major problem. There is some evidence of Executive dominance in legislation yet this can be justified when it is considered that it is the Executive's responsibility to suggest legislation for the good governing of NI. Equally, scrutiny has been enacted at times with very damaging results for the Executive and this does indicate that while the Executive may have the upper hand some of the time, it cannot avoid Assembly scrutiny all of the time.

### LEARNING OPPORTUNITY

Students should carry out a mock investigation in which one student plays the part of the relevant departmental minister and the others play the role of the committee. All should be fully prepped on the matter to be discussed and all of the relevant political parties should be represented.

## Representation in the NI Assembly

The third key function of the Assembly is to ensure that the views of the electorate are accurately represented in legislation produced, and that constituency and other interests are addressed in the chamber.

MLAs are primarily elected on the basis of their party designation, with the exception of independents, who may also hold seats in the Assembly. This means that MLAs have a requirement to represent the views of that party. They may also want to represent the views of a cause or special interest which is dear to them, or in which they have a deep-rooted interest.

Above all, however, MLAs should be representing their constituency, because these are the people who elected them, and ultimately the people who can decide in a future election to remove them from office.

This section will consider how MLAs carry out this role, although in contrast with the other two sections, it is much more difficult to come to any firm conclusion as to how well they do this. At best, by trying to ascertain how much of an MLAs time is, on average, spent on constituency matters, it is possible to draw conclusions from that as to their overall performance as constituency representatives. The following list gives an idea of the various ways MLAs can carry out their representative role. Some of these will be familiar, as they are also methods for carrying out their legislative or scrutiny roles.

### *Ways in which MLAs can carry out their representative role*

1.  Raising a constituency issue at Question Time, through a written question to a minister, or by holding an adjournment debate on the matter.
2.  Making sure that constituency concerns, either for the physical area or for the needs of individuals or groups within the constituency, are taken into consideration in new legislation, by playing an active role in debates and in the line-by-line analysis of legislation during the committee stage.
3.  Introducing a Private Member's Bill to address an issue raised by a constituent, or to help the constituency in general.
4.  MLAs can also join All Party Groups (APGs) to look at issues relevant to constituents. These are not formally part of the Assembly and are made up of MLAs and outside organisations who share an interest in a particular issue. Although they have no formal role in the Assembly, they are fast becoming an important part of the process. They allow MLAs to make the necessary connections

with other groups to make sure that, when they raise issues in the Assembly, they are better informed than if they were just working on an issue on their own. There are currently thirty-five APGs.

5.  In addition to these roles in the Assembly, MLAs, as part of their representative role, are expected to carry out a number of roles in their constituency. These include: holding surgeries, which afford constituents an opportunity to raise issues and problems for the MLA to address; acting as a local dignitary by opening new facilities or attending school events; making sure that the facilities in the area are maintained and that new investment is attracted to the constituency; acting as a spokesperson; and acting as an ambassador for the constituency.

### How effective are MLAs as representatives?

It is hard to evaluate the effectiveness of MLAs in this area, though the regular watching of either Assembly debates or Ministers' Question Time will reveal that MLAs do frequently raise constituency matters and, for the most part, spend a lot more time in their constituency working on local matters than most people are aware of. Undoubtedly, some are better than others at this role, and the best MLAs are those who try to represent all of their constituency, regardless of whether certain areas within it would be likely to vote for them.

As a result of having five MLAs for each constituency,[11] there should be ample representation, and MLAs do encourage members of the public to contact their offices for advice and help. As in the UK, most of the time MLAs deal with complaints about other government services. The most common complaint is about health services, followed by education, but MLAs may have to deal with a wide range of issues, and a good MLA will be ready to act on behalf of their constituents across a range of issues. The bigger parties also have an advantage here (as they do in other areas) as they tend to have bigger constituency offices, more staff – both paid and voluntary – and therefore more people to actually get things done. This means they can sometimes appear to be much more in touch with the electorate and more prepared to work for the area. This brings its own rewards, as good constituency workers are much more likely to hold on to their seat.

In a broader sense, MLAs are very socially representative of the electorate, unlike the UK parliament, which tends to be dominated by university-educated, white, male and middle-class members. However, there is still a problem with the under-representation of both women and ethnic minorities at Stormont, though the class background is varied and reflects the grass-roots nature of many of the political parties. Some of these issues will be explored in more detail in Chapter 4, which deals with political parties and elections.

## KEY TERMS

**Cross-community voting** – A form of voting designed to ensure that a measure has majority support from both of the main communities. There are two ways this can happen: parallel voting or weighted majority. It is a safeguarding measure used for key decisions, and can be triggered by a Petition of Concern.

**Petitions of Concern** – A procedure designed to prevent discriminatory laws being passed. It requires at least thirty MLAs to sign a petition, which will then require a measure to be designated a key decision, requiring it to have a cross-community vote in order to pass.

**Accelerated Passage Procedure** – A procedure available to the Executive, which permits a bill to be 'pushed through' quickly by skipping the committee stage. It is not supposed to be used frequently, and is designed for dealing with emergencies. It was used 17 times between 2011 and 2016.

**Private Member's Bill** – Also known as a Non-Executive Bill, this is one suggested by an individual MLA. Although there have been relatively few passed so far, there is evidence (from the Assembly Bill Office) to suggest that MLAs are becoming more comfortable with this aspect of their role, and that there will be more in the future.

**Forward Work Plan** – The plan used by Statutory Committees to guide their work for each Assembly session.

## What do MLAs do?

In short, MLAs perform all of the various functions already reviewed: they carry out the representative, legislative and scrutiny functions in the Assembly. In order to do this, they take part in Assembly debates and votes; ask, and in some cases answer, pertinent questions; and participate in committees and the line-by-line scrutiny of legislation. In addition, they hold inquiries and pursue research into their own pet projects and legislative initiatives. They also have a party role, which means they will have party duties to perform, both at Stormont and in their local area.

There is a public perception that MLAs are overpaid and underworked, yet a look at the average MLA's diary, or indeed a more informed account of the various roles they must perform, would call this view into question. Professor Wilford is of the opinion that they barely have enough time to perform all of their duties, which hardly indicates that they are underworked[12] – in fact, quite the opposite. When the Assembly is sitting, the majority of MLAs spend Monday to Thursday at the Assembly working on a variety of tasks, all related to the three key functions identified earlier.

This is reflected in the structure of the weekly Assembly timetable, which sets aside Monday and Tuesday for full or plenary meetings for legislative debates; questions for ministers and for the First Minister and deputy First Minister; and opportunities for adjournment debates. Wednesdays and Thursdays are set aside for committee business, and since committee meetings last for two to three hours at a time, and most MLAs belong to three committees, this can take up the best part of these two days. Fridays are set aside for constituency work, as is also the case in the rest of the UK; and MLAs are expected to attend constituency surgeries and address constituent grievances as best they can.

It is tempting, when there is a lot of negative press surrounding the Assembly (for example, during prolonged periods of inactivity such as in 2017), to conclude that MLAs do not do enough – to suggest that they spend too much time on tribal politics and do not seem able to move fully on from the past. There are some very important questions which need to be asked about the way MLAs use their powers, and if they are actually representing the people who elected them, or if they are more concerned with their party view. However, these are questions common to most legislative assemblies and their members, and not specific to NI. The reality is that most MLAs are very busy, spending a lot of time working behind the scenes trying to get good quality legislation passed, Executive and otherwise, and making sure that the quality of government is the best it can be.

A visit to the Assembly makes it clear that in spite of media images to the contrary, MLAs tend to collaborate well with each other and perform their roles in a professional and focused manner. The majority of MLAs work over sixty hours per week, which is far in excess of the public perception of their role.

### Final remarks
To recap then, the three key functions of the Assembly are representation, legislation and scrutiny, and there is some debate about how well the Assembly

carries out these functions. These include criticisms of the Petitions of Concern procedure, and debate about the planned reforms of this and other Assembly procedures.

The Assembly has already undergone a fairly radical degree of reform since the number of MLAs was dropped from 108 to 90, and it has been argued that this will make it more difficult for MLAs to carry out all of their roles effectively. On the other hand, the 2016 reform of the Executive Committee, and the reduction in the number of departments from twelve to nine, means there are fewer Statutory Committees and therefore fewer committees needing members. The result of all of these reforms, and any future changes to the Assembly, need to be monitored and assessed, and all need a period of operation before any firm conclusions can be reached.

### Endnotes

1   Strand 1, Article 1, Point 1, *The Belfast Agreement*, 1998

2   Strand 1, Article 1, Point 4, *The Belfast Agreement*, 1998

3   In the original GFA there were 108 MLAs, 6 for each of the constituencies. This was reduced in 2017 in line with proposed structural changes, which included the reduction in government departments.

4   Prior to the reduction in overall number of MLAs (from 108 to 90) in 2017, the DUP had 38 seats in the Assembly and Sinn Féin had 28. For the DUP in particular this change meant they no longer had the numerical strength to launch a Petition of Concern if a measure they disagreed with came up for vote.

5   Dr Alex Schwartz of Queen's University School of Law is one of the most dedicated and articulate critics of the device. He applies his expert knowledge of constitutional law to the issue and has produced a series of excellent articles on the subject, some of which can be found at www.qpol.qub.ac.uk/the-problem-with-petitions-of-concern/

6   More on this can be found in, Birrell, Derek *Comparing Devolved Governance* (Palgrave Macmillan, 2012)

7   The Assembly Education service provides up-to-date information on its website and in publications sent electronically to schools, which helps provide detailed evidence to support some of the points being made in this section. In addition senior civil servants have played a significant part in delivering teacher training events at Stormont specifically for those involved in teaching GCE Government and Politics. These events give an invaluable insight into the complex way statutory committees work.

8   Wilford, Rick, quoted in Peter Cheney, 'Under the Whip' from *agendaNI Magazine*, 28 January 2011, www.agendani.com

9   Wilford, Rick. Paper presented at the A/AS-Level Teacher Training Conference, 11 October 2016, Stormont Parliament Buildings.

10  Not be confused with the BBC political television programme of the same name.

11  There were six up until 2017.

12  Wilford paper, October 2016, *op. cit.*

# POLITICAL PARTIES
# AND ELECTIONS

# Political Parties and Elections

This chapter will be largely focused on the policies and electoral performance of the largest political parties in NI – the Democratic Unionist Party (DUP), Sinn Féin, the Social Democratic Labour Party (SDLP), the Ulster Unionist Party (UUP) and the Alliance Party. The chapter will begin with a brief account of their reaction to, and role in, the Good Friday Agreement; their policies; their electoral performance since 1998, and the reasons for this. The chapter ends with a section on the smaller political parties to allow for an analysis of a variety of perspectives, and to acknowledge those who have played a significant role in the past and present.

### The political parties and the Good Friday Agreement

**The Social Democratic and Labour Party:** The SDLP are, arguably, the reason the Good Friday Agreement came about in the first place. They worked tirelessly behind the scenes to secure the trust of both the British government and the IRA that negotiations for a new political solution were worth investigating. This began with John Major's government and was continued by Labour, when Tony Blair took over as prime minister in 1997. John Hume and Seamus Mallon (SDLP leader and deputy leader) had the confidence of the British authorities and they persuaded both the IRA and the British government to meet up to discuss the possibility of a negotiated political solution. These 'talks about talks' were the first step on the road to devolution. The SDLP were, therefore, in many ways the most enthusiastic supporters of the GFA and, with hindsight, this appears to be the highpoint in their political history thus far. By the time of the St Andrews Agreement, they had been politically eclipsed by Sinn Féin, and as a result did not play a leading role in that agreement. They continue to struggle to regain their electoral status as the main nationalist party, as Sinn Féin have gone from strength to strength.

**The Ulster Unionist Party:** The UUP were one of the key groups involved in the original negotiations and in drafting the GFA. They were arguably the only voice for unionism, as the DUP refused to participate, and therefore were under a lot of pressure. Although they remained the dominant force within unionism following the signing of the GFA, and provided the first ever First Minister, David Trimble, they ultimately paid the price for aspects of the agreement that were unpalatable to the unionist community – issues such as the failure to secure prior decommissioning of the IRA, the NSMC and proposed reform of the RUC. The DUP were able to exploit this discontent, in order to maximise their own support. Many unionist voters changed allegiance to the DUP, and the UUP lost their position as the main voice of unionism. They have continued to fully support the Agreement and, although they did not play a significant role in the renegotiation at St Andrews, they have welcomed the changes it brought.

**The Democratic Unionist Party:** The DUP refused to take part in negotiations and staged a protest outside Stormont in the final days leading up to the signing of the Agreement. Once it was signed, they took their seats with the aim of undermining it from within. They tried to do this by rotating ministers, obstructing meetings and refusing to cooperate with the NSMC. Over time they changed this policy so that, by 2002–3 they were talking about working for a renegotiation rather than a complete abandonment of the Good Friday Agreement. This reflected their growing electoral support. They played a key role in the renegotiation at St Andrews, and have given the Good Friday Agreement full and complete support ever since.

**Sinn Féin:** It was clear at the time of the GFA that Sinn Féin were facing a difficult balancing act between fully embracing all aspects of the Agreement and keeping their more hard-line supporters on board, yet they played a full role in the negotiations. It was essential for the success of the agreement that Sinn Féin convince the IRA that the war was over, and this partly explains why there was so much of a delay concerning decommissioning of IRA guns. Although this was not a requirement before the setting up of the first Assembly and Executive, it quickly became a sticking point for the whole peace process, and was the reason for a number of suspensions. Ultimately it was to cost the UUP their electoral position as the main unionist party. This was a tricky issue for both unionists and Sinn Féin, as unionists believed that Sinn Féin were really planning to rearm and re-launch the armed struggle from a stronger position; whereas for the Sinn Féin leaders, it was important not to push their supporters too far too quickly. Indeed, there was some opposition to the Good Friday Agreement from within republicanism, expressed today in the dissident republican movement. Sinn Féin played a full role in the St Andrews Agreement and have been working well within the devolved institutions ever since.

**The Alliance Party:** Alliance supported the GFA and all of its institutions from the time of signing and have continued to do so ever since. They have welcomed some of the changes which resulted from St Andrews, and have played a bigger role since the Hillsborough Agreement 2010, which saw the devolution of Policing and Justice to NI. The Alliance Party's David Ford became the first ever NI justice minister due to the party's uniquely middle of the road approach, much to the consternation of the SDLP, who, statistically speaking, should have got the role.

Therefore, we can see that the political parties have changed their attitude to devolution since 1998. The most obvious change in direction has been from the DUP, who have gone from being completely opposed to devolution to fully endorsing it and playing the lead role in the institutions. The UUP have moved from full support to a more qualified support, believing that power sharing, in both the Executive Committee and the Assembly, favours the two main parties and alienates smaller parties, and that an official opposition would make the system better. The SDLP, like the UUP, have criticised the tendency of the two main parties to dominate the others and, in tandem with the UUP, think an official opposition is beneficial. Alliance are supportive of the institutions, and see them as a necessary part of an ongoing peace process. However they, too, are concerned that NI has become a dyarchy and, following the 2016 Assembly election, chose to give up the justice ministry in order to go into opposition alongside the UUP and the SDLP. Sinn Féin are enthusiastically operating the institutions, and although there have been differences between themselves and their main coalition partners, the DUP, they have made a success of the institutions and associated bodies.

## NI political parties' reaction to the Good Friday Agreement
The following table summarises the ways the five main parties have changed their views on the institutions and on the GFA. This can be used to help students organise their ideas and as the basis for a mini-essay as part of their exam preparation.

|  | **Reaction to Good Friday Agreement** | **How has this changed and what has stayed the same?** |
|---|---|---|
| DUP | **Opposed**<br>Led the 'No' campaign outside Stormont during negotiations and, after the Agreement was signed, during the referendum that followed.<br><br>Then members took seats believing they could destroy it from within (by rotating ministers, refusing to speak to Sinn Féin and refusing to take part in NSMC). | Once they became the biggest unionist party, they worked for a renegotiation (St Andrews) and came to accept power sharing and devolution, working well in both the Executive and the Assembly.<br><br>Still want to stay in the UK but are more prepared to work with the Republic of Ireland.<br><br>Still very opposed to cultural challenges (e.g. want Parades Commission closed down; opposed to the flag only being flown on designated days; took a while to support policing changes etc.)<br><br>New strong opposition to gay marriage and are right-wing on moral issues. |
| Sinn Féin | **In favour**<br>Worked well in negotiations and in pre-negotiations. | Most of their significant change in policy was prior to the Agreement – from armed struggle to democratic means.<br><br>Prepared to take seats in the Assembly but not Westminster (some change in abstentionist policy).<br><br>Still very much a united Ireland party and the only one to have candidates in both NI and RoI elections. |

| | Reaction to Good Friday Agreement | How has this changed and what has stayed the same? |
|---|---|---|
| UUP | **In favour**<br>As the biggest unionist party at the time, were key negotiators in, and supporters of, the Agreement.<br><br>Lost unionist support for going into government with Sinn Féin before IRA decommissioning. | Still support the Agreement but criticise the lack of a formal opposition, as they say it makes the Executive too strong.<br><br>Have become more unionist and hard-line to try to win back support. |
| SDLP | **In favour**<br>Arguably the party most responsible for the agreement. Brought Sinn Féin in from cold; key part of talks and negotiations; fully support power sharing with Irish dimension. | Claim there needs to be an official opposition to stop Executive dominance. Still support the Agreement, but have become more nationalist and hard-line in an attempt to win back seats from Sinn Féin. |
| Alliance | **In favour**<br>Always in favour and have not changed approach. However, some concern with regard to the Agreement entrenching the sectarian divide. | No real change. |

**LEARNING OPPORTUNITY**

Students should use the table above to write two pages on how the views and policies of the parties have changed regarding the Good Friday Agreement and the devolved institutions, since 1998.

## The main policies of the political parties

Party policies are constantly evolving and often the policies noted on the party websites reflect their most recent election campaign, which can be confusing for students. If there has been a local council election, for instance, very specific local policies, such as refuse collection, will be highlighted on the party website and not more regionally applicable policies. On the other hand, if there has been a European election then the policies will reflect the party view on the EU and details on how the party will make sure NI gets a good deal from EU membership (although, following Brexit, this will no longer be a concern).

The range, and recently the frequency, of elections can make the task of identifying party policies a difficult one for both teachers and students. The aim is to get a good overview of the main policies, similarities and differences, between the parties without getting too tied down in very specific details. As with other political systems it can be useful to use the terms 'left- and right-wing' to help categorise the party beliefs, however it will become apparent that NI parties do not adhere to this dichotomy as readily as parties in other parts of the UK.

All parties change and develop over time, circumstances change, the economy and attitudes change and if parties are to survive and to continue to represent the people that elect them they need to change too. This rate of change is often gradual and it can be easy to assume knowledge of a party's stance on an issue when in fact it may be very different.

All of the main parties have demonstrated change since the signing of the GFA. The DUP have significantly changed their attitude to power sharing, the NSMC and working with Sinn Féin. However, they are still very committed to defending the union, maintaining a strong British identity in NI and on upholding a socially conservative stance on moral or social issues such as abortion rights or same-sex marriage. Sinn Féin have changed in their attitude on these social issues, going from opposing the 'right to choose' to supporting it under certain circumstances, and championing LGBT rights by means of the equal marriage act. Both parties have shown, through their work in the Executive, an ability to work well together, get over old differences and come up with common aims and policies. They have taken a pragmatic approach to implementing the welfare reforms required by the Westminster government, even though both don't particularly like these reforms (Sinn Féin are vehemently opposed to them). Nonetheless agreement has been made and the reforms are being implemented. They have also both agreed to suspend the enactment of water charges in NI and to maintain a commitment to the shared education programme.

The other parties have also changed their policies over time in response to the needs of their voters, and in accordance with their vision of what would be good for NI. For example, the Alliance Party originally regarded same-sex marriage as a matter of conscience for individual members, but subsequently changed this policy and now supports the measure. The SDLP have moved to support integrated education, a major move for what is widely seen as a Catholic middle-class party. Similarly, the UUP demonstrated a more progressive stance in the run up to the 2017 Assembly election, calling for a change in attitude towards same-sex marriage and asking UUP voters to consider voting SDLP in their second preference vote.

Often a party's first policy area – usually a more controversial or traditional issue such as the constitutional status of NI – will be its main priority, though it will, of course, have policies in many different areas. The following tables do not cover all those policies, but will focus on the five main areas – the economy, health, education, social issues, and constitutional/legacy issues – giving a broad outline of each party's current stance. These areas are not addressed in any particular order, and the tables do not necessarily reflect the order in which the parties address these issues, but they give a selection of the main areas to allow for comparison and analysis.

## Key policy areas

### The Economy

| | |
|---|---|
| DUP | • Promote tourism as a key growth area<br>• Identify other key areas for growth such as the agri-food industry and the creative industries<br>• Create 50,000 jobs<br>• Encourage more apprenticeships<br>• Reduce corporation tax to 10 per cent<br>• Improve provision of childcare |
| Sinn Féin | • Tackle disadvantage<br>• Identify tourism, agri-food and creative industries as growth areas for the economy<br>• Create 50,000 jobs<br>• Support the reduction in corporation tax to 12.5 per cent<br>• Transfer of full fiscal powers to Stormont<br>• Commitment to putting people at the heart of the economy, by ensuring that it serves society by providing adequate education, housing and welfare, and equitably redistributing wealth |

| UUP | • Support manufacturing<br>• Identify tourism, agri-food and creative industries as growth areas for the economy.<br>• Support the reduction in corporation tax to 12.5 per cent<br>• Reduce air passenger duty<br>• Improve golf tourism |
|---|---|
| SDLP | • Increase jobs<br>• Focus on growth industries: agri-food, ICT, tourism<br>• Improve provision of childcare |
| Alliance | • Focus on job creation and skills<br>• Reduce regulation for small businesses<br>• Support key growth industries: agri-food, ICT, tourism |

These policies show a fair degree of overlap, particularly those of the DUP and Sinn Féin, reflecting their position as the dominant parties in the Executive. There are differences too, for example on the Sinn Féin website there is a very socialist feel to some of the policy statements on the economy. All parties recognise that there are growth areas in the NI economy, which are in the tourist, agri-food, ICT and creative industries, and most commit to helping growth in these areas.

## Health

| DUP | • Pledge £1 billion to health service<br>• Identify the need to recruit more GPs and provide them with more support<br>• Improve mental health services<br>• Reduce waiting lists<br>• Encourage active and healthy ageing |
|---|---|
| Sinn Féin | • Pledge £1 billion to health service<br>• Provide free healthcare for all<br>• Prioritise disability services and mental health services<br>• Increase GP intake at universities<br>• Involve all health workers in decision and planning |

| | |
|---|---|
| UUP | • Improve mental health services<br>• Identify the need to recruit more GPs and provide them with more support<br>• Improve cancer care<br>• Decrease waiting lists<br>• Improve preventative medicine<br>• Increase training on and awareness of dementia leading to earlier diagnosis |
| SDLP | • Improve mental health provision<br>• Identify the need to recruit more GPs and provide them with more support<br>• Increase support for healthcare staff<br>• More support to those with conflict-related trauma and other mental illnesses |
| Alliance | • Develop preventative strategies<br>• Identify the need to recruit more GPs and provide them with more support<br>• Target obesity, drug and alcohol abuse<br>• Address mental health issues<br>• Address social care for elderly |

From these policies we can see unanimous support for improved mental health services, and recognition that there is a disproportionate need in this area in NI.[1] All of the parties identify the need to support GPs, the primary caregivers in the Health Department. There is an increasing crisis in GP provision in NI and this growing problem is reflected in the policies of the five main parties, which are committed to helping GPs or trying to recruit more.

Each party also has unique areas of interest within healthcare, such as the Alliance Party identifying the growing social care problem arising from an ageing population, or the UUP identifying the need for better dementia services. Interesting again to note that the two biggest parties in the Executive mirror each other with a pledge of £1 billion for the NI health service by 2020.

## Education

| | |
|---|---|
| DUP | • Support shared education<br>• Introduce one common transfer test for primary school leavers<br>• Supports keeping university tuition fees at current rate and keeping Education Maintenance Allowance (EMA)<br>• Support early years provision<br>• Remove need for Catholic Teacher Training Certificate to teach in Catholic primary schools |
| Sinn Féin | • Retain EMA<br>• Freeze student fees<br>• Support Irish-medium schools<br>• Invest in schools in areas of high social deprivation<br>• Increase parental choice |
| UUP | • Remove right of Catholic primary and nursery schools to only hire teachers who have the Catholic Teaching Certificate.<br>• Devise new transfer method for primary school leavers<br>• Committed to funding further and higher education, opposed to rise in cost of higher education<br>• Committed to maintaining EMA |
| SDLP | • Support a reduction of university fees<br>• Support integrated education<br>• Critical of shared education scheme<br>• Support further education and EMA |
| Alliance | • Committed to integration – aiming for 20 per cent of children to be in integrated education by 2020<br>• Supports keeping university tuition fees at current rate and keeping EMA for students<br>• Aim to pilot a targeted program for numeracy and literacy in schools.<br>• Committed to spending all the childcare budget (they argue that DUP and Sinn Féin did not do this) |

The biggest difference between the parties centres on the replacement for the eleven-plus transfer test. Sinn Féin and the SDLP remain committed to removing testing at age eleven as far as possible, whereas both the UUP and

DUP support the grammar school system and would like to see a new transfer method in place as soon as possible. There is also a disparity between those who support shared education and those who support integrated education. These are very different educational systems, with shared education being based on efficiency and sharing of resources between schools and integrated education a dedicated attempt to remove the long-standing religious segregation in our school system. All of our parties are committed to keeping student fees low, maintaining EMA and making education as accessible as possible for all.

The main parties had a high degree of overlap on the preceding policy areas, however it is in the next areas that a wider disparity can be seen. The first of these, social issues, has seen a high public profile particularly amongst the young. On no other policy area is the generation gap more evident and this throws up interesting issues for the more conservative parties.

## Social Issues

| DUP | • Oppose extending UK abortion rights to NI<br>• Oppose extending UK right to same-sex marriage to gay couples in NI |
| --- | --- |
| Sinn Féin | • Allowances for abortion can be made under certain circumstances<br>• Support same-sex marriage |
| UUP | • Offer members a conscience vote on abortion rights<br>• Oppose same-sex marriage[2] |
| SDLP | • Oppose extending UK abortion rights to NI<br>• Moved to supporting same-sex marriage under leadership of Colum Eastwood |
| Alliance | • Offer members a conscience vote on abortion rights<br>• Support same-sex marriage[3] |

In this area we can see considerable disparity between the more traditional parties and new smaller parties; and some difference from unionist and nationalist perspectives. Unionists tend to come out as the more socially conservative of the two traditional political blocks, with nationalists being more likely to see both abortion and same-sex marriage as equality issues.

However, the SDLP remain very strongly opposed to the extension of abortion rights to NI so this is not always the correct conclusion. New, smaller parties such as People Before Profit and the Green Party are in favour of both of these measures, and the same-sex marriage bill was originally put forward in the Assembly in 2011 by Stephen Agnew (Green Party).

## Constitutional and Legacy Issues

| | |
|---|---|
| DUP | • Committed to maintaining the union<br>• Support dismantling the Parades Commission<br>• Believe the Union flag should be flown at civic offices all year long<br>• Opposed to implementation of Irish Language Act<br>• Failed to enact legacy aspects of SHA<br>• Failed to bring in a pension for those severely injured in the conflict<br>• Adhere to a limited definition of 'victim' |
| Sinn Féin | • Committed to a united Ireland<br>• Support the Parades Commission<br>• Support restrictions on flying the Union flag and on the flying of loyalist paramilitary flags<br>• Fully support Irish Language Act<br>• Failed to enact legacy aspects of SHA<br>• Support a pension for all those injured as a result of the conflict, including those injured while carrying out an act of terrorism<br>• Support a broad definition of term victim, which gives recognition to those affected by the state as well as those affected by paramilitary activity |
| UUP | • Committed to maintaining the union<br>• Support dismantling of Parades Commission<br>• Believe solution to 'flag protest' is being flexible regarding when the Union flag is flown<br>• See no need for an Irish Language Act at this time<br>• Support the legacy measures set out in the SHA<br>• Support the need for a pension for those severely injured in the conflict<br>• Define victim according to definition used in 2000 Terrorism Act |

| | |
|---|---|
| SDLP | • Committed to a united Ireland<br><br>• Support Parades Commission<br><br>• Support view that Union flag should be flown on designated days only<br><br>• Support implementation of Irish Language Act<br><br>• Support the enactment of the legacy aspects of the SHA<br><br>• Support the need for a pension for those severely injured during the conflict<br><br>• They take a broad definition of victims, and would like policy makers to have more direct contact with victims |
| Alliance | • Support consent principle as in GFA<br><br>• Support work and role of Parades Commission<br><br>• Believe Union flag should only be flown on designated days, in accordance with the rest of UK<br><br>• Support the implementation of an Irish Language Act<br><br>• Support legacy measures in SHA<br><br>• Would like broad definition of victim and support listening to victims directly<br><br>• Called on Executive to solve the pension issue as soon as possible to ease suffering of those involved |

It is in dealing with the constitutional and past/legacy issues that there is often the greatest disparity among the parties and, unsurprisingly, this reflects the very different aims and experiences of the two sides of the community. Some of these issues are definitely worth more in-depth consideration, as they frequently seem to hold up political dialogue. Sometimes NI politicians seem to be out of sync with the electorate with regards to these matters, and that can cause frustration amongst the people. In the main, however, these are important and emotive issues because they are deeply related to identity. Any notions of contested identity, or perceived threats to identity, acquire a potency that makes them difficult to resolve.

It is clear then, that all the parties have changed their policies over time, and a more detailed inspection of each party's manifesto is recommended. The DUP have moved from being avowedly anti-Agreement to being the main partner in the Executive. Sinn Féin's endorsement of the Policing Board and relaxation of their abstentionist policy to take seats in Stormont were also significant policy changes. The SDLP, UUP and Alliance Party have all had to adapt in a very difficult political terrain as their more moderate standpoints have sometimes led to a loss of votes.

## The electoral performance of the main parties

Before looking at the actual electoral performance of the various parties, it is helpful to understand the basics of the two electoral systems used in NI elections: first-past-the-post, used for general or Westminster elections; and proportional representation, used for local council and Assembly elections. However this is purely for the purposes of deeper understanding and it is not an area that will be examined, unlike the performance of political parties, which will.

### NI's two electoral systems

**First-past-the-post (FPTP)** is a simple majority system, and is the same method used in the UK. It is an easy system, both to use and understand: on their ballot paper, electors place an 'x' beside their preferred candidate. This system, however, is associated with an unfair divergence between votes cast and seats gained. In short, it makes it harder for smaller parties to gain seats and favours two or three big parties. For this reason, it is not regarded as a good option for systems where there are deep divisions in society, and where distortions between votes cast and seats gained would be problematic.[4]

**Proportional Representation** was the system put in place for local assembly elections at the time of the Government of Ireland Act 1920. The system used then and now was PR-STV (Single Transferrable Vote), which was designed to try to make the percentage of votes cast mirror the percentage of seats gained as closely as possible. PR-STV is associated with coalition government, which makes it unpopular for systems used to strong one-party government (like the UK), but given that coalition is mandatory for NI's devolved institutions, this is not an issue. Both the use of PR-STV and the mandatory coalition are key features of consociationalism and therefore the electoral system is a key part of NI's political system, and its operation.

PR-STV allows voters to order their selection of candidates in preference – usually from 1 to 5 – although electors can, in theory, rank as many or as few of the candidates as they prefer. Each constituency has a quota of votes required in order to secure a seat. As Assembly constituencies are multi-member (in other words, have five seats available), first preference choices are counted until that quota of votes is reached, and then votes are allocated to second preference votes, and so on. The process continues until all five seats have been filled.

The Assembly Education Service has some excellent material on the details of the process, including worked examples, and is well worth a look.[5] However, students are not expected to be able to explain this in any detail in the exam, and it is simply for background knowledge. The main thing to remember is that PR-STV is the system used for Assembly elections because it is fairer and more suitable for a divided society, whereas FPTP is used for Westminster or General Elections.

### The electoral performance of the five main parties 1998–2017

The focus of the exam will be on the performance of the five main parties in the Assembly elections, but it is equally useful, when tracking how a popular or unpopular a party is becoming, to refer to Westminster elections. For this reason, both will be referred to.

Due to the tribal nature of politics in NI, competition between the main unionist and nationalist parties focuses on trying to win votes from their communal rivals. In other words, unionists are trying to get the most unionist votes and nationalists are trying to get the most nationalist votes. This means that when analysing their electoral performance, the focus will be on why one unionist party is more popular than the other and likewise, why one nationalist party is more popular than the other. Political scientists call this 'internecine conflict' or conflict within the group, and it is important for students to be clear that, if they are asked to explain the

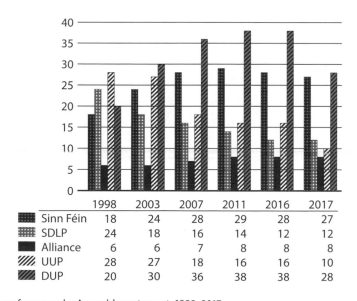

|  | 1998 | 2003 | 2007 | 2011 | 2016 | 2017 |
|---|---|---|---|---|---|---|
| Sinn Féin | 18 | 24 | 28 | 29 | 28 | 27 |
| SDLP | 24 | 18 | 16 | 14 | 12 | 12 |
| Alliance | 6 | 6 | 7 | 8 | 8 | 8 |
| UUP | 28 | 27 | 18 | 16 | 16 | 10 |
| DUP | 20 | 30 | 36 | 38 | 38 | 28 |

Electoral performance by Assembly seat count, 1998–2017

electoral performance of a unionist or nationalist party, they will need to refer to the fortunes of other parties within that community if they are to give a full account. The same does not apply to non-tribal parties, or to the new emerging parties such as the Green Party or People Before Profit. In these cases, it is more important that students can trace and explain why these new parties are emerging and what it says about politics in NI.

## DUP

In 1998, in the first Assembly election, the DUP got 18.5 per cent of the vote and 20 seats. By 2003, this had risen to 25.7 per cent and 30 seats, and by 2011 it had risen further to 30 per cent and 38 seats, making them by far the biggest party in the Assembly. This meant that, from 1998 to 2011, the DUP went from being the fourth party to being the largest. The turning point came in 2003 when, for the first time, they were convincingly ahead of the UUP. In that election the UUP got 22.7 per cent of the vote and the DUP 25.7 per cent. In the 2017 elections, the DUP polled 28.1 per cent and 28 seats.

The DUP saw a similar increase in their vote at Westminster. In 1997 the party had 2 seats, in 2001 they had 5 seats, and in 2005 they had 9 seats. The 2010 Westminster election saw the party retain 9 seats but lose Peter Robinson's East Belfast seat to Naomi Long (Alliance Party). In 2015 they had 8 seats, but in 2017 they had 10 seats. This increase led to the DUP playing a key

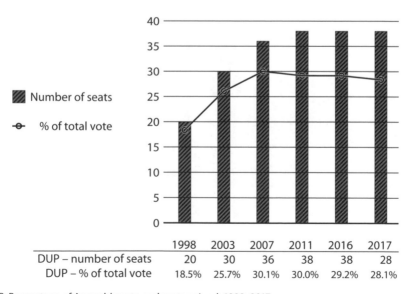

| | 1998 | 2003 | 2007 | 2011 | 2016 | 2017 |
|---|---|---|---|---|---|---|
| DUP – number of seats | 20 | 30 | 36 | 38 | 38 | 28 |
| DUP – % of total vote | 18.5% | 25.7% | 30.1% | 30.0% | 29.2% | 28.1% |

DUP: Percentage of Assembly vote and seats gained, 1998–2017 role in the formation of Theresa May's new government. A hung parliament – the Conservative Party got 42 per cent of the vote, 318 seats; Labour got 40 per cent, 262 seats – meant that the Conservatives needed the DUP's support. The parties entered into a 'confidence and supply' arrangement in which the DUP would support the government on certain issues, such as Brexit and the policies outlined in the Queen's speech, but it falls short of a full coalition.

## UUP

In the first Assembly election, 1998, the UUP got 21.3 per cent of the vote and 28 seats, coming in second to the SDLP by percentage votes (SDLP received 22 per cent) but not in seats, hence the reason David Trimble was First Minister, not John Hume. In the 2007 election, this dropped again to 14.9 per cent, compared to the DUP's 30.1 per cent; and they hit an all-time low in 2011, dropping to become the fourth largest party in NI, with only 13.2 per cent of the vote. They have held that position in subsequent elections, receiving 12.9 per cent of the vote and 10 seats in the 2017 Assembly election.

This decline is reflected even more drastically in the Westminster elections. In 1997 the UUP were the largest single party in NI, polling 32.7 per cent of the vote and holding 10 Westminster seats. However by 2001 they held only 27 per cent of the vote, and in 2003 this dropped again to 23 per cent when they were overtaken by the DUP (25 per cent). as the voice of unionism in NI. Today they have no Westminster seats at all.

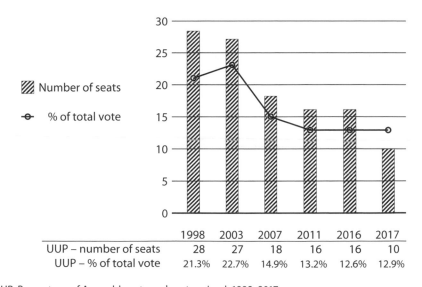

| | 1998 | 2003 | 2007 | 2011 | 2016 | 2017 |
|---|---|---|---|---|---|---|
| UUP – number of seats | 28 | 27 | 18 | 16 | 16 | 10 |
| UUP – % of total vote | 21.3% | 22.7% | 14.9% | 13.2% | 12.6% | 12.9% |

UUP: Percentage of Assembly vote and seats gained, 1998–2017

## Reasons for DUP success/UUP decline

The electoral performance of the two main unionist parties is inextricably linked – the DUP's rise correlates with the UUP's fall, and the significant change in support for the two parties has to take into account a number of factors. From an analyst's point of view, these factors can be broken up into distinct sections: political circumstances; leadership; policies and strategy.

In order to account for the changing electoral patterns within unionism, all of these areas should be considered, with attention being given to how both of the main unionist parties have been affected by the various factors.

- **Political circumstances:** Unionists were dissatisfied by some of the GFA's terms – in particular, the failure to establish decommissioning prior to Sinn Féin taking their seats, the plans to reform the RUC, and the early release of prisoners – and tended to blame the UUP for this. This helped the DUP, who were seen by unionists as 'standing up' to Sinn Féin. The more successful Sinn Féin became, the more threatened unionists felt, and they turned to the DUP to represent their position and get a better deal for their community.

- **Leadership:** The UUP went through several leaders in order to try to regain votes. David Trimble (leader, 1995–2005) lost credibility over the GFA and his initial reaction, to try to play the 'Orange' card and become a bit more hard-line, did not work. He resigned following the 2005 Westminster elections, when the UUP lost five out of six seats.

  Trimble was replaced by Reg Empey (leader, 2005–10), who tried to create a broader unionist group at the Assembly by including the Progressive Unionist Party (PUP). However, this backfired and caused dissension within the UUP. He then tried an alliance with the Conservatives in order to regain votes, and in the 2010 Westminster election fought under the banner of UCUNF (Ulster Conservatives and Unionists: New Force). This election saw the UUP lose all of their Westminster seats and Empey resigned.

  He was replaced by Tom Elliott (leader, 2010–12), who turned the party to the right, ended the alliance with the Conservatives and reverted to playing the 'Orange' card. After a number of PR disasters – such as referring to some elements of Sinn Féin as 'scum' during his victory speech – more members of the UUP left and the party's electoral performance continued to decline.[6] In 2012, following the

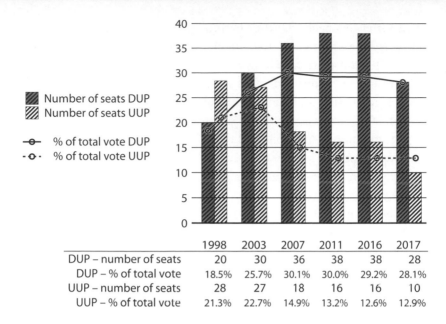

| | 1998 | 2003 | 2007 | 2011 | 2016 | 2017 |
|---|---|---|---|---|---|---|
| DUP – number of seats | 20 | 30 | 36 | 38 | 38 | 28 |
| DUP – % of total vote | 18.5% | 25.7% | 30.1% | 30.0% | 29.2% | 28.1% |
| UUP – number of seats | 28 | 27 | 18 | 16 | 16 | 10 |
| UUP – % of total vote | 21.3% | 22.7% | 14.9% | 13.2% | 12.6% | 12.9% |

UUP and DUP performance in Assembly elections, 1998–2017

disastrous 2011 Assembly elections, which saw the UUP vote drop to 13.2 per cent, Elliott was replaced by Mike Nesbitt (leader, 2012–17) who stepped down after the party's poor showing in the 2017 Assembly elections. He was replaced by Robin Swann.

The DUP, on the other hand, benefitted from the strong leadership of Ian Paisley (leader, 1971–2008). He had a long-standing reputation and proven track record of opposing republicanism. When he resigned, he was succeeded by Peter Robinson (leader, 2008–15), his long-standing deputy, and one of the most senior members of the DUP. Robinson led the party to successive victories and projected a business-like manner during his time as leader, despite having some difficult terrain to navigate.[7] Robinson's successor, Arlene Foster (leader, 2015–present), saw the DUP through the successful 2016 Assembly election and, despite subsequent difficulties and scandals, has established a reputation as being a strong and solid leader.[8]

- **Policies and strategy:** Ironically, Paisley's successful leadership of the anti-GFA campaign was one of the reasons for the DUP's subsequent rise to dominance, and resulted in the amazing development in 2007, when he and Martin McGuinness took over as First and deputy First

Ministers, respectively. They had such a good relationship that they earned the nickname 'The Chuckle Brothers'.

This drastic change in policy reflects the degree to which the DUP were able to change and adapt with the circumstances, while retaining their reputation as the main unionist defenders. The decision to form an Executive with Sinn Féin only came after the St Andrews renegotiation of the GFA, and the DUP could claim credit for forcing this to happen. Since 2007, they have benefitted from being the main party in the Executive, and both the DUP and Sinn Féin now look like the parties of government just because they have held the dominant positions in the Executive since this time. The successful operation of devolution has been associated with them, rather than with the UUP and SDLP, their more moderate counterparts, who led the Executive during the long period of stop-start devolution and suspensions.

Arguably, the most important factor has been the way in which the DUP moved from outright opposition to the GFA to embracing devolution and producing solid policies focused on broader issues than the old sectarian flag-waving policies with which they are traditionally associated. While remaining strong on the union, and on attacking the IRA (and at times, Sinn Féin), they have also developed a broad manifesto, which demonstrates their commitment to moving forward.

## Sinn Féin

In 1998, in the first Assembly election, Sinn Féin got 16.7 per cent of the vote – an increase from the Westminster elections of the previous year, when they got 16 per cent. This has been interpreted as the electorate attempting to encourage the party to embrace peace. In the next Assembly elections in 2003, they got 23.5 per cent, overtaking the SDLP as the dominant nationalist party (the SDLP got 17.0 per cent). By 2007, Sinn Féin's Assembly vote had risen to 26.2 per cent, by 2011 this was at 26.9 per cent, securing them 29 seats in the Assembly, and in 2017 they got 27.9 per cent, and 27 seats.

This success rate has been mirrored in Westminster elections: in 2001 they got 22 per cent of the vote; in 2005 this rose to 24 per cent; in 2010 this rose again to 25.5 per cent of the vote, securing the right to take 5 seats at Westminster. The most recent Westminster election saw their vote go up to 29.4 per cent, giving them 7 seats. These results effectively wiped out the SDLP vote and secured Sinn Féin's position as the dominant nationalist party.

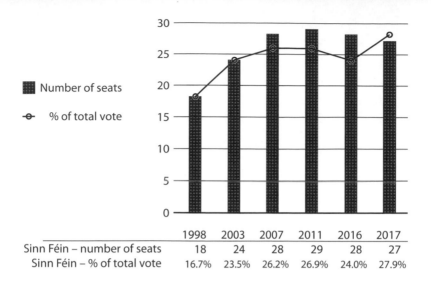

| | 1998 | 2003 | 2007 | 2011 | 2016 | 2017 |
|---|---|---|---|---|---|---|
| Sinn Féin – number of seats | 18 | 24 | 28 | 29 | 28 | 27 |
| Sinn Féin – % of total vote | 16.7% | 23.5% | 26.2% | 26.9% | 24.0% | 27.9% |

Sinn Féin: Percentage of Assembly vote and seats gained, 1998–2017

## SDLP

In the 1998 Assembly elections, the SDLP polled the highest percentage of votes of all the NI parties (22.0 per cent) yet have seen their votes steadily and dramatically eroded in favour of Sinn Féin, their more hard-line counterparts, and are now the third largest party, with just 12 seats. Like the UUP, they are struggling to find their role in the post-GFA devolved system, which they were so central in creating. The second Assembly election in 2003 marked the transfer of nationalist support from the SDLP (17.0 per cent) to Sinn Féin (23.5 per cent). In 2007, the SDLP recived just 15.2 per cent of the vote, Sinn Féin, 26.2 per cent; in 2011 this dropped to 14.2 per cent and Sinn Féin, 26.9 per cent. Then, in the 2017 Assembly election, the SDLP's result dropped to 11.9 per cent and Sinn Féin's vote rose to 27.9 per cent.

In Westminster elections, they have seen a similar decline – from 21 per cent in 2001 to 16.5 per cent in 2010, although because of how their votes are scattered, they initially managed to retain the three seats they had held since 2001. This changed in 2017 when they lost all of their Westminster seats as a result of a catastrophic fall in votes to 11.7 per cent.

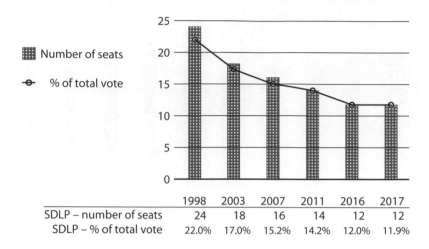

| | 1998 | 2003 | 2007 | 2011 | 2016 | 2017 |
|---|---|---|---|---|---|---|
| SDLP – number of seats | 24 | 18 | 16 | 14 | 12 | 12 |
| SDLP – % of total vote | 22.0% | 17.0% | 15.2% | 14.2% | 12.0% | 11.9% |

SDLP: Percentage of Assembly vote and seats gained, 1998–2017

### Reasons for Sinn Féin success/SDLP decline

As with the DUP/UUP, the decline of the SDLP and the rise of Sinn Féin are undoubtedly connected, and so will be considered as part of the same topic. Amazingly, from their high point in 1998, the SDLP have lost out to Sinn Féin in every election since and, as Sinn Féin are now associated with being in power, this makes it harder for the SDLP to gain credibility.

- **Political circumstances:** Sinn Féin gained votes from 1996 onwards as the nationalist community tried to encourage them to keep on the path to peace. People who would never have voted for Sinn Féin when they actively supported armed struggle showed their willingness to support them when this was given up, and a ceasefire was declared. Sinn Féin have built upon that initial platform ever since.

- **Leadership:** Sinn Féin have had a solid leadership in NI, with people like Gerry Adams (overall party leader, 1983–present) and Martin McGuinness (NI political leader, 2007–17).[9] They commanded respect from their colleagues, and had a clear vision of where they wanted the party to go. McGuinness' successor, Michelle O'Neill (NI political leader, 2017–present) is a solid negotiator, her first task being to head the party team in their 2017 negotiations with the DUP (to set up a new Executive following the election).[10]

By contrast, the SDLP have had recurrent leadership problems ever since John Hume (leader, 1979–2001) and Seamus Mallon (deputy leader, 1979–2001) retired. Mark Durkan (leader, 2001–10) had a largely uncontentious time as leader, although he grew increasingly critical of the DUP and Sinn Féin and what he regarded as their monopoly of power. Margaret Ritchie (leader, 2010–11) was blamed for the party's poor performance in the 2011 Assembly elections and, like Durkan, stood down in order to concentrate on her Westminster career. Alasdair McDonnell (leader, 2011–15) got off to an inauspicious start when he complained about the lighting at his victory press conference. The party replaced him, after four years in office, with Colum Eastwood (leader, 2015–present), in an attempt to modernise the party image and give some new direction.

- **Policies and strategy:** Sinn Féin have been much better than the SDLP at getting supporters out to attract voters, door to door. From the early 1990s, they would provide cars and drivers for those too ill or elderly to get to the polling stations. They were more visible around election time, partly because their supporters were younger and less middle-class, and so had more free time to devote to party work. They were also better at maintaining a high profile in areas, and would often be the first party to address issues important to local communities (for example, they had ramps put in to residential areas to help reduce the problems caused by joyriders). They have a well-developed system of advice centres and would rarely be unavailable for those seeking advice. Gradually, through this level of constituency dedication, they were able to win over even the most reluctant nationalist voters.

    Sinn Féin also have a clear and detailed set of policies, which have showed development but also consistency. They are the only party to openly and actively address the underrepresentation of women in politics in NI and have put their women's equality strategy into practice (they have far more female MLAs and members than any of the other parties). They are firmly seen as the 'equality' party, marketing themselves as the party of the working class, and have overtaken the SDLP in both the youth and working-class vote.

    The SDLP, on the other hand, look older and seem more out of touch than Sinn Féin. They seem a lot less progressive on women's issues, and on other social issues in general. Their image is too middle class, which, given they are the sister party of the British Labour Party, seems unfair. In responding to this, they have resorted to 'greening up' their image in an attempt to stave off the Sinn Féin onslaught. This has not helped them, and they now seem unsure of their identity. Furthermore, their target vote is unlikely to be impressed by blatant attempts to out-republicanise Sinn Féin.

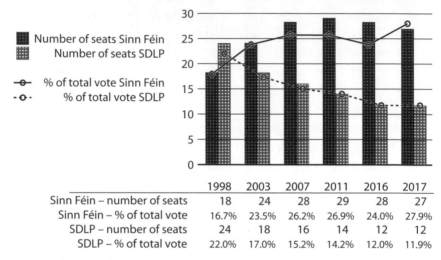

| | 1998 | 2003 | 2007 | 2011 | 2016 | 2017 |
|---|---|---|---|---|---|---|
| Sinn Féin – number of seats | 18 | 24 | 28 | 29 | 28 | 27 |
| Sinn Féin – % of total vote | 16.7% | 23.5% | 26.2% | 26.9% | 24.0% | 27.9% |
| SDLP – number of seats | 24 | 18 | 16 | 14 | 12 | 12 |
| SDLP – % of total vote | 22.0% | 17.0% | 15.2% | 14.2% | 12.0% | 11.9% |

Sinn Féin and SDLP performance in Assembly elections, 1998–2017

## Alliance

In the 1998 Assembly elections, Alliance got 6.5 per cent of the vote and 6 seats. In 2003 this dropped to 3.7 per cent, but they still got 6 seats. In 2007 there was a slight increase when they got 5.2 per cent and 7 seats. In 2011, they got 7.7 per cent and 8 seats (a slow and steady increase). In the 2017 Assembly election, Alliance got 9.1 per cent of the vote, which saw them retain the 8 seats they already had.

In Westminster elections, Alliance got 3.6 per cent of the vote in 2001, and 3.9 per cent in 2005, rising to 6.3 per cent in 2010, which got them one seat, held by Naomi Long. She lost the seat by a narrow margin in the 2015 election – largely because the unionist parties united to field one unionist candidate – and many Alliance supporters remain hopeful that this seat will be regained in the future.

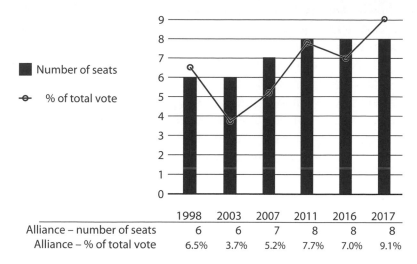

| | 1998 | 2003 | 2007 | 2011 | 2016 | 2017 |
|---|---|---|---|---|---|---|
| Alliance – number of seats | 6 | 6 | 7 | 8 | 8 | 8 |
| Alliance – % of total vote | 6.5% | 3.7% | 5.2% | 7.7% | 7.0% | 9.1% |

Alliance: Percentage of Assembly vote and seats gained, 1998–2017

### Explaining the Alliance vote

The fortunes of the Alliance Party have only fluctuated slightly over the years, despite the recent increase in their public profile. They have had a long struggle to see major electoral gains and, although their position in Stormont could be described as fairly steady, it is worth considering why the party has struggled to gain higher votes – not least because this could be a popular question in the final exam. There are a number of possible explanations:

- **Political circumstances:** The party was doing well until 1981, but took a notable downturn after the polarisation in politics which followed the hunger strikes. During particularly polarised periods, voters revert to more extreme tribal parties, which results in a drop in votes for more moderate parties. Alliance, along with other more moderate parties, have suffered as a result of this.

- **Leadership:** Seán Neeson (leader, 1998–2001) was the first Alliance leader following the signing of the GFA. He took over at a difficult time for the party and was heavily criticised for his 2001 electoral strategy. He was replaced by David Ford (leader, 2001–16) who successfully led the party for fifteen years and raised the party profile significantly when he was justice minister. His successor Naomi Long (leader, 2016–present) has overseen a growth in the Alliance vote and is well positioned to take the party forward.

- **Policies and strategy:** The party is seen as middle class, and policies such as lowering the corporation tax, albeit with the aim of attracting more inward investment, reinforces this view.

There is also a very regional-specific aspect to the Alliance vote – it does very well in Belfast and has in fact seen rises in its Belfast-based support (for example, 2011 saw 35 per cent of the party's total support come from the Greater Belfast area, and a similar result was seen in 2016). Correspondingly, the Alliance have very little support west of the Bann, and this concentration of their vote by area may well make it difficult for them to increase their overall vote without targeting these areas specifically.

One of the key issues is that, although the party has always made a concerted effort to attract votes from all parts of Northern Irish society, it is designated as unionist in the Assembly, which has led to a steady decline in votes from the nationalist community.

For a time this corresponded with a growth in support from amongst moderate unionists, however, the party's role in the 2012 flag debacle has also potentially alienated unionist voters. Rather ironically, as they have moved more towards a liberal and non-sectarian approach, Alliance have risked losing their core support group.

It also seems that, although the party *has* become more associated with the liberal tradition, and the UK Liberal Democrats in particular, they still seem to lag behind most liberal parties with regard to their policies. In the recent same-sex marriage debate in the Assembly, not all Alliance MLAs supported the motion – a surprising response from a party wishing to draw a distinction between itself and the other parties, and trying to establish its good liberal credentials.

## LEARNING OPPORTUNITY

Students should draw up a table for each of the five main parties indicating how they have performed across a range of elections, how their policies have changed, how and why their leaders have changed, and reasons for success or failure. This is a significant but worthwhile task and lends itself well to group-based learning.

## The smaller parties, past and present

Although the main focus of the specification and exams will be on the main or bigger parties, a number of smaller parties – such as the NIWC and the PUP, who had a brief flowering during the early years at Stormont – have played a role in the development of the peace process, the drafting of the Good Friday Agreement, and operation of the early part of devolution, and they deserve to have some acknowledgement.

## UK parties

Both the Conservative and Labour Parties stood candidates in the 2016 Assembly elections and it was interesting to see their results. The Conservatives had been trying to make inroads into the unionist vote over a number of elections, and did see a small 0.4 per cent rise in support, attaining 2,554 first preference votes. Not groundbreaking by any means, but a small increase nonetheless. For the Labour Party, this move was a break with mainstream UK Labour Party policy and the first time the Labour Party had stood in an NI Assembly election. They attained 1,577 first preference votes, which corresponds to 0.2 per cent of the vote. In the subsequent 2017 Assembly election, only the Conservatives stood candidates and they gained 2,399 first preference votes. The Northern Ireland Labour Representation Committee, the name given to the Labour Party branch standing for election in NI, decided not to put forward any candidates.

## NI Women's Coalition (NIWC), 1996–2006

The NIWC was originally founded in 1996 by Monica McWilliams and Pearl Sagar (joint leaders, 1996–2006), with the aim of gaining seats in the forthcoming peace negotiations, and with three core principles – equality, human rights and inclusion. They got 1 per cent of the vote and gained 2 seats at the peace negotiations.

In spite of experiencing a high level of verbal harassment and being subjected, throughout the process, to an oppressive attitude from the other delegates, the NIWC made a significant contribution to the negotiations, not least because they took a totally different approach to that of the traditional parties.[11]

The two areas that benefitted most from the NIWC presence at the talks were rights and reconciliation. The party brought both a unique perspective and a scholarly and hardworking attitude to the preparation of papers and responses, something, which it has been claimed, was absent from the other parties. It could be said that, outside of academia, the contribution of the

NIWC to both the negotiations and the final agreement has not been properly acknowledged. They were the only party to prepare detailed papers informed by international research on peace processes elsewhere (for example, they cited the South African model particularly with regard to how it had handled gender issues) and many of the ideas they suggested were incorporated into the final agreement.

It was the NIWC who suggested there should be fresh inquiries into historically controversial events such as Bloody Sunday, and 'The Disappeared', as part of confidence building and dealing with the past. They also put forward proposals for the support of both victims and prisoners which, in both cases, reflected their strategy to try to reintegrate marginalised groups back into the community. In addition, they suggested that people in NI should be able to opt for Irish, British or dual citizenship as a way of getting around the national identity problem.

Following the discussions, two members of the NIWC were elected to the first Assembly – Monica McWilliams and Jane Morrice – and the party's influence was felt on several occasions. For example, they suggested that both family-friendly hours and childcare expenses for MLAs should be provided, and this was taken on board. They spoke out in favour of divorce reforms, which other parties were slow to endorse, with many making impassioned pleas on the sanctity of marriage. Similarly, it was the NIWC representatives in the Assembly who introduced the first Private Member's Bill calling for the establishment of a Children's Commissioner. This was eventually passed by means of an Order in Council, during the period of suspension in 2003.

The NIWC suffered from a general polarisation in politics which crept in after the suspension and resulted in the two extreme parties, DUP and Sinn Féin, gaining prominence, and they lost both of their Assembly seats and ceased to operate as a political party shortly afterwards.

### Progressive Unionist Party (PUP), 1979–present

The PUP was formed in the 1970s as a small left-orientated unionist party, whose main aim was to give a voice to working-class Protestants in some of the most socially deprived areas of Belfast. It was linked to loyalist paramilitary groups, the UVF and the Red Hand Commando (RHC).

The party was founded by Hugh Smyth (leader, 1979–2002) and attracted David Overend and Jim MacDonald, who had been members of the NI Labour Party. Overend is believed to be responsible for many of the early manifestos which reflect the party's left-wing approach to socio-economic issues – the PUP has always openly supported abortion (unlike all the other parties), equality for women and support for environmentalism – while being committed to maintaining the union. Its two best-known members are David Ervine (leader, 2002–07) and Dawn Purvis (leader, 2007–10), and its current leader is Billy Hutchison (leader 2011–present).

The PUP were at the negotiating table for the GFA and they gave the Agreement full support, including a commitment to decommissioning. In 1998, they polled 1.6 per cent of the vote – enough to secure two Assembly members, Hutchison and Ervine. In 2007, however, Hutchison lost his North Belfast seat, although the party did have a very active and effective MLA in the form of Dawn Purvis, who replaced the by then deceased party leader in East Belfast. However, Purvis resigned from the party in 2010 in a row about continued links to active paramilitary groups. The party has seen a decline in support since then, and has failed to secure any representation in the Assembly.

The PUP played a role in opening up dialogue and debate within loyalism, with Ervine in particular being associated with a genuinely progressive attitude. The party has stayed loyal to its roots as a left-wing loyalist party, working more on socio-economic issues. It supported same-sex marriage in 2013, and is the only unionist party to firmly do so. It is against zero-hours contracts and has continued to be a party which advances the ability and rights of women to play a full role in politics.

The problem for the PUP is regaining the support of the Protestant working class from their direct rivals, the TUV and the DUP. It is proving hard for the PUP to retain their dwindling support, and it looks very much like they may have passed their electoral peak.

## The Green Party, 1985–present

The Green Party are a non-sectarian, left-wing party with approximately 700 members, and are one of the new and growing parties in NI politics. Standing on a progressive platform, they have four key values: social justice, environmental sustainability, grass-roots democracy and non-violence. They also have a distinct LGBQT branch called the Queer Greens, and, in 2011, were the first party to bring forward legislation on same-sex marriage in the Assembly. They have campaigned for children's services to be improved, and in 2015, this saw the successful passage of a Private Member's Bill brought up by Steven Agnew (leader, 2011–present).

The party has its roots in the NI Ecology Party, which was set up in the early 1980s by Ecology candidates Peter Emerson, Avril McCandless and Malcolm Samuels.[12] In 1985, the party changed its name to the Green Party, in line with other European ecology parties. In 2007, in recognition of a growing interest in green politics, and the need for alternatives to traditional parties in NI, Queen's University established a Green Society, which has acted as a stimulus for debate ever since.

The party is relatively new to electoral politics but has shown a steady increase in votes. From 2007–17 they held 1 seat in the Assembly, and this increased to 2 in the 2017 elections – Clare Bailey and Steven Agnew. A second Assembly election in early 2017 nearly cost Bailey her seat, but she captured the public and media imagination in what was dubbed 'staying up for Bailey' as pundits watched the South Belfast returns until the early hours of the morning to see her retain the seat.

The party's Westminster vote has also seen a sizeable increase over the years – in 1997 they secured 0.1 per cent (539 individual votes); in 2015 this rose to 1 per cent (6,822 votes); and in 2017 their vote went up to 7,452.

### Traditional Unionist Voice (TUV), 2007–present

This party was founded in 2007 as an anti-St Andrews splinter group from the DUP. Currently led by Jim Allister (leader, 2011–present), the party is opposed to mandatory coalition, committed to the union, is socially conservative and dedicated to upholding the rule of law. It is also resolutely against working with Sinn Féin, and still regards the GFA and subsequent St Andrews revisions as a betrayal. Its members are highly critical of the other unionist parties, accusing them of abandoning their principles so they can get into government.

The party, as with most extreme parties, often attracts publicity for all the wrong reasons, yet, despite their often controversial policies, Allister has a dedicated following. He has carved out a name for himself at Stormont, through a mixture of shock at some of his more extreme presentiments and admiration for what is often seen as straight talking. His reputation is that of the lone opposition in the Assembly, and he will take on all sides of the house, as has been seen on numerous occasions.

Regular viewers of televised Stormont sessions will get to know him quite quickly, as he is a key player within the chamber. Even among those who would never dream of voting for the TUV, there is an admiration for some of his frank and no-nonsense comments. His criticisms of other parties can be very accurate, and this is not missed by the electorate, and his more severe remarks are often forgiven as a result of this.

In the 2010 Westminster elections, the TUV were disappointed not to have received more votes. However, Allister had taken on Ian Paisley, Jnr in his North Antrim constituency, and gained a very respectable 7,000 votes, compared to Paisley's 19,000. In the 2017 Assembly election the party saw its share of the vote drop slightly again to 2.6 per cent. This was a drop of 0.9 per cent, however the party still secured 20,523 first preference votes and succeeded in holding one seat in the Assembly.

Overall, the party's future success really will depend on whether it can capitalise on unionist discontent with the more mainstream unionist parties, or if the DUP is able to convince unionist voters that their vote is safe with them.

## The People Before Profit Alliance (PBP), 2005–present

PBP, with its system of collective leadership, operates on an all-Ireland basis and has been slowly building an electoral profile in the Irish Republic since its formation in 2005. One of its members, Gerry Carroll, successfully gained a seat in the Belfast City Council in 2014, but it was the party's victory in the 2016 Assembly elections that is most impressive.

Carroll saw an astonishing success in West Belfast when he topped the poll with the majority of first preference votes, and received the resounding success that comes with being the first candidate elected in the constituency. His success was all the more surprising given the usual predominance of Sinn Féin in West Belfast, and demonstrated some indication of dissatisfaction with that party. But his was not the only victory. In the same election, PBP's Eamonn McCann, a long-standing and well-known local socialist and commentator, took a seat for the Foyle constituency, while a third candidate for the party did very well in North Belfast – Fiona Ferguson gained 3.5 per cent of first preference votes, or approximately 1,832 votes in total.

However, the 2016 success of the party has been regarded as a protest vote, which will lack longevity. Indeed in the 2017 election, PBP saw a reduction in their vote and the loss of Eamonn McCann's seat.

## United Kingdom Independence Party (UKIP), 1991 (2012 in NI)–present

There was one UKIP MLA in the Assembly until 2016, David McNarry, who started as a UUP MLA and was first elected to the Assembly in 2003. He was suspended by UUP leader Tom Elliott in 2012, and joined UKIP later that year.

In the 2015 Westminster elections, UKIP performed well, gaining 18,324 votes, and the party was hopeful that it would be able to see its support grow in tandem with the growth experienced by UKIP in the rest of the United Kingdom. It was proud of being the only party with representation in all parts of the UK, and hoped that its anti-immigration and anti-EU policies would help them secure a niche in the discontented unionist vote.

McNarry criticised the Assembly for spending too much time on social issues rather than economic matters. Unlike the TUV, however, UKIP are much less socially conservative and, although McNarry expressed the view that too much time was spent debating issues such as gay marriage and abortion, he recognised that these were important issues, especially for those affected by them directly.

UKIP have also raised the profile on homelessness and patient care issues, and have therefore shown themselves to be about more than just getting the UK and NI out of Europe. They played an active role in the pro-Brexit campaign in NI in the run-up to the 2016 referendum, and were delighted by the result. The 2016 Assembly elections saw McNarry (the only UKIP MLA) lose his seat, and the party currently has no representation in the Assembly.

## Final remarks

The purpose of this chapter was to provide a summary of the development, policies and electoral performance of the main parties that regularly compete in NI elections. Policies and electoral performance of parties will change, and this is perhaps the section of the system that is the most dynamic and prone to change. Students of politics need to be constantly vigilant, via the media and current political debate, to keep on top of the state of play with the political parties.

### Endnotes

1 A study conducted by the Commission for Victims and Survivors, concluded that 213,000 people in NI (a staggering proportion of the population) had a diagnosed mental health issue as a direct result of the conflict. The SDLP refer to this research specifically in their policy.

2 However, some UUP members are in favour, e.g. Andy Allen.

3 For years Alliance were split on the issue of same-sex marriage, and allowed a conscience vote on it.

4 In a divided society this can increase the political power of the already presiding party and result in a system in which they perpetually dominate – as was the case in NI, 1921–72.

5 See www.niassembly.gov.uk for more information.

6   Harry Hamilton and Paula Bradshaw both left to join the Alliance Party over disagreements about Elliott's leadership and the direction in which he was taking the party.

7   In January 2010, his wife, Iris Robinson, was embroiled in scandal when a BBC NI documentary revealed that she had been involved in an extramarital affair.

8   Rumours circulated that her relationship with deputy First Minister, Martin McGuinness was strained and difficult. Then in early 2017 the RHI scandal, McGuiness' resignation, and the subsequent collapse of the institutions led to widespread criticism and a heavy media onslaught.

9   At the time of print, Adams had just announced he would step down as Sinn Féin leader in 2018.

10  O'Neill's appointment was a first for the party in a number of ways. Not only is she the first woman to lead the party but she is also the first leader with no direct IRA past.

11  For more information on the difficulties referred to, see Ward, Margaret, 'The Northern Ireland Assembly and Women: assessing the gender deficit', Democratic Dialogue (December 2000).

12  Emerson is one of the longest-serving 'green' candidates, standing on an ecology platform in North Belfast in 1977. He is a well-known figure in North Belfast, and his commitment to green politics is beyond question.

13  Tonge, Jonathan, Comparative Peace Processes, (Polity Press, 2014), 6

# Conclusion

There has been a lot of criticism of the NI political institutions and of MLAs in the media and amongst the public at large. One of the things that should be understood about the devolved institutions is that they are part of a peace *process*. They are a stage on a journey to peace and mark one section of the process rather than being the end game in themselves.

One of the problems when assessing the political institutions is avoiding the temptation to expect all forms of sectarianism and remnants of the pre-1998 conflict to have totally disappeared just because there is an Assembly. This isn't realistic and we must accept that there will be ongoing challenges.

Political scientist Jonathan Tonge describes this process: "Acceptance of the term 'peace process' requires understanding that transitions towards non-violence and the permanent eradication of conflict are non-linear, subject to regression and rarely short." He points out that peace processes are slippery, with hard-to-define finishing points but recognisable stages. In common with other peace processes in similarly divided societies, the recognisable stages can be mapped as follows:

- Secret exploratory dialogue.
- Public discussions and negotiations.
- Achieving a peace deal.
- Resolution of the divisions which caused the conflict – long term.
- Management of the divisions and the underlying problems that precipitated violent conflict.[13]

By this estimation NI is currently at stage 4/5 and at times seem to still struggle with aspects of the process. By recognising that the devolved institutions and their associated sets of compromises – such as early prisoner releases or involvement of ex-combatants in the new political processes – are part of a process, we can start to be a bit more realistic about what can be achieved and how.

The real test will be in how well the institutions deal with the management of old divisions while trying to meet the demands of new challenges. The maintenance of peace is reliant on all of the main groups seeing a real benefit to peace, but this isn't always clear in the current economic climate and will prove challenging. In post-conflict societies there is a potential problem with a rise in crime and gangsterism, which in the context of NI could destabilise the process.

Furthermore, as can be seen with the difficulties the institutions have had dealing with legacy issues, there needs to be some way of dealing with the past. Reconciliation and healing through truth-telling have been a part of the successful resolution of conflicts elsewhere, most notably in Bosnia and South Africa, and there are lessons to be learned from these processes if Northern Ireland is to move forward. However, all of these matters are issues that arise in all post-conflict societies and in this sense should be expected.

What we have seen since 1998 is an evolving process. The original Good Friday Agreement has been updated and expanded upon by St Andrews, Hillsborough Castle and Stormont House. There have been reforms to the institutions, which include reducing the number of MLAs, the number of Executive departments and introducing an official opposition. Protagonists such as Sinn Féin and the DUP have been able to find common ground, while MLAs are increasingly demonstrating their ability to display a professional and responsible attitude. New political parties are emerging and, although these may find attaining seats in an Assembly reduced to 90 seats a struggle, they do add new voices to the arena of debate, which in itself is a welcome addition.

In the midst of all the negativity it is good to try to keep sight of what has been achieved and to avoid falling into the trap of repeating media headlines and instead apply a rigorous academic eye to the accuracy of these interpretations.

# Glossary

The following is a list of key terms that you should be able to use and explain confidently.

**Ad Hoc Committee:** a temporary Assembly Committee that is formed to deal with one specific issue.

**Assembly:** the NI parliament or legislature is called the Assembly. It is currently made up of 90 MLAs and sits at Parliament Buildings in the Stormont estate.

**Authority:** the right to rule or to exercise power usually derived from consensus in liberal democracies. This is usually provided by adherence to democratic practices, such as winning elections and observing the rule of law.

**Boundary Commission:** A group set up to consider and finalise the Irish border in 1925.

**Consensus:** an agreement among a group of people.

**Consociational:** a form of democracy considered ideal for divided societies. It has four key features: mutual veto; proportional system of voting; power-sharing Executive; and guarantees of cultural equality. All of these features are key aspects of the Good Friday Agreement and are based on successful consociational models elsewhere.

**Constituency:** the geographical area which each MP or MLA represents. In the case of MLAs, there will be six representatives for each constituency, as required by the consociational model of democracy followed in NI.

**Democracy:** a system of government which is said to derive power from the people. The common usage of the term could more accurately be seen as a definition of a representative democracy, which is a form of democracy where the people elect their representatives, thereby giving them the power to make decisions on their behalf in the parliamentary system.

**Democratic deficit:** the term used to describe a lack of democracy in a supposedly democratic system. Used in reference to the way NI was ruled under direct rule, and associated with the passing of laws using Orders in Council.

**Devolution:** the redistribution of power to a regional parliament or assembly, allowing that assembly to make decisions which will affect the people who live there. A devolved assembly will have designated areas which it has control over and others which it does not. There are three devolved institutions within the UK: the Welsh Assembly, the Scottish Parliament and the NI Assembly.

**D'Hondt system:** the system used to allocate seats in local elections in NI. This method uses a quota system which involves counting first preference votes, applying the relevant quota and awarding seats, then recounting and reapplying the quota until all six seats in a constituency have been awarded. It is also used to allocate the chairs of committees and the ministerial posts in the Executive Committee.

**Direct Rule:** the ruling of NI directly from Westminster, imposed as a result of the breakdown of law and order in NI, and the increasing belief that the Stormont government was unable to control the situation.

**Dyarchy:** rule by two independent groups. This is also referred to as double government.

**Executive:** the part of the political system which is referred to as the government, and which makes the plans and policies for the parliament or legislature to decide upon. It is the job of the Executive to come up with a vision for the way forward, and then to try to get this through.

**First-past-the-post system (FPTP):** the system of election used in the UK and in NI for general elections. It is a more straightforward system than PR-STV, but it also results in a higher distortion of the votes/seat ratio. In other words, the percentage of the vote received is not necessarily reflected in the percentage of seats gained in parliament, and smaller or third and fourth parties find themselves disproportionately losing out in this system.

**Gerrymandering:** this refers to the practice of artificially drawing electoral boundaries in a way which favours one group over another.

**Good Friday Agreement (GFA):** the Agreement which laid down the terms for the operation of the devolved institutions and the framework for consociationalism in NI. Also known as the Belfast Agreement.

**Intergovernmental Conference:** this was set up under the Anglo-Irish Agreement to allow cooperation between the British and Irish governments on matters of mutual interest. It was replaced in 1998 with the British-Irish Intergovernmental Conference.

**Joint Committee:** a committee meeting which allows members from more than one committee to attend, usually to consider a matter which affects more than one area.

**Legislative role:** the ability to pass and influence legislation. This is often seen as the primary role of MLAs and other parliamentarians – hence the term legislator, indicating the importance of the law-making aspect of their function.

**MLA:** Member of the Legislative Assembly, the official title for the elected Assembly representatives in the NI devolved institutions.

**MP:** Member of Parliament, strictly speaking, could be considered to refer to both members of the House of Commons and Lords. However, it is more commonly used to denote a Member of the House of Commons in the UK system of government.

**Nationalist:** a term used to describe someone whose political beliefs are based primarily on their national identity and aspirations. In the case of NI, the term relates mainly to those parties and individuals who have a strong Irish identity, and desire to see an end to partition, and the reunification of the island of Ireland.

**Parallel consent:** a way of making sure that contentious issues in the NI Assembly receive cross-community support. This method requires that 50 per cent of the members present support the matter, and that it also gets 50 per cent of unionist and 50 per cent of nationalist support.

**Petition of Concern:** designed to prevent discriminatory legislation being passed, a Petition of Concern is a parliamentary device unique in the UK to the NI Assembly. It allows 30 MLAs to have a measure designated as a key decision, which will make it more difficult to pass.

**Power:** the ability to influence others or to control outcomes. Political power refers specifically to the ability to decide where resources will be allocated and which policies will be enacted.

**Power sharing:** a form of government favoured in ethnically divided societies, which requires opposing political groups to come together in a grand coalition in order to govern more fairly.

**Proportional representation:** an electoral method which results in a better correlation between votes cast and seats awarded. It uses a quota system and multi-member constituencies. A feature of consociational democracy.

**Quango:** a body which is set up by the government to carry out a government policy. An example of a quango is the Public Health Agency.

**Representative role**: one of the key roles of MLAs is to represent the interests of the people who voted for them. They will also represent the interests of their party and of groups they personally support, such as Shelter or Age Concern.

**Scrutiny function:** the scrutiny function is a key aspect of a democratic system. It allows MLAs to ask questions of the Executive, to make sure they are acting within the limits of the law and in the best interest of the public.

**Single transferable vote:** the type of proportional representation which is used in NI to elect MLAs and MEPs.

**Speaker:** the person whose job it is to keep order and call MLAs for debate and questions.

**Standing Committees:** these are the six permanent committees set up to deal with the day-to-day business of the devolved institutions.

**Statutory Committees:** these committees carry out both a legislative and a scrutiny role, and have an extensive range of powers to be able to carry out their roles effectively.

**Unionist:** a term used to describe someone whose political views are based primarily on their strong belief that the best interests of NI lie in maintaining the union with Britain. The term relates mainly to those parties and individuals who share this belief and have a strong British identity.

**Weighted majority:** a method of voting in the NI Assembly, which requires 60 per cent of all those voting to support the measure under consideration and 40 per cent of both nationalists and unionists present and voting in favour of the motion.

# Exam Guidance

Exam success begins well before the date of the exam, and the aim of this final section is to help students to prepare as thoroughly as possible for the AS Government and Politics of NI exam by focusing on how best to approach the questions.

An incredibly useful activity is to go through the past papers and use these to draw up a list of possible questions from which you can then create question plans. It is a good idea to do this with a study partner as two heads are definitely better than one, when it comes to essay-planning in particular, and it will make the activity more interesting.

You can then practice **timed** unseen answers, which will give you the best training for the exam. Use past papers for this activity or, in the case of the new specification where there are no actual past papers, use papers from the previous specification as the next best thing. The topic headings below have been listed with suggested subsections for revision purposes below:

### The Four Agreements
Background to Good Friday Agreement
- How was NI governed under direct rule?
- What was wrong with this?
- What is meant by the term democratic deficit?
- What political events led to the Agreement?

The Four Agreements – constitutional arrangements for NI
- What are the provisions of the Good Friday Agreement?
- How did St Andrews change this? What did it add? Why was it needed?
- What did the Hillsborough Agreement do, and why?
- What are the constitutional and political implications of the Stormont House Agreement?

### The Executive Committee
The Executive Committee – the government of NI
- How is the Executive Committee chosen?
- What is the Executive Office and what does it do?
- What do ministers do?
- What are the main functions/purpose of the Executive Committee?

- Can the Executive Committee dominate the Assembly?
- What restrictions are there on the powers of the Executive Committee?
- How effectively have the Executive Committees carried out their role since 2007?
- Have the various Executive Committees since 2007 been able to operate a power-sharing system in spite of continued divisions?

### The Northern Ireland Assembly

The Northern Ireland Assembly – the parliament of NI

- What are the main roles/functions of the Assembly?
- What does the speaker do?
- What do MLAs do and how are they elected?
- How effective has the Assembly been as a legislative body since 2007?
- How effective has the Assembly been as a scrutiny body since 2007?
- How independent is the Assembly from the Executive?
- How can MLAs carry out their representative role both in and outside of the Assembly?
- How and why are Assembly Committees so important?
- What are Petitions of Concern and why are they proving controversial?

### The Northern Ireland Political Parties

The political parties and elections

- What was the reaction of the five main political parties to the Good Friday Agreement?
- How have these views have changed over time?
- What are the current policies of the main five parties – the DUP, the UUP, Alliance, the SDLP and Sinn Féin?
- What has been the electoral performance of the five main parties since 1998 and what were the reasons for this?
- How do the main parties both agree and disagree?
- What are the policies of the smaller parties (TUV, the Green Party, UKIP and NIWC)? What are their policies? How they are performing? How have they contributed to the political process in the past?

## How to approach the exam questions

There are **50** marks available for this paper in total. Every single mark matters and you should focus on trying to get the maximum number of marks for each question in order to increase the total marks. You will have to answer four questions from a possible five. The questions are staggered in the level of difficulty and therefore the marks correspondingly increase as the paper progresses. The layout, as demonstrated in the specimen subject assessment materials on the CCEA website (www.ccea.org.uk), is as follows:

**Question 1** (4 marks) – Straightforward identification of two items in order to gain total marks. Answer this question by providing two clear identifications. If you are struggling for a second, then guess rather than miss an opportunity to pick up marks. There are no marks for explanation in this question, so do not waste time by giving one – two straightforward identifications will suffice. For example, if the question asks for two ways an MLA can influence legislation, then stating 'Private Member's Bill' and 'voting' will gain the full four marks.

**Question 2** (6 marks) – A correct identification, with full explanation and an appropriate example is necessary to access the full marks. Answer this question by defining the term or matter in the question, then explain it as fully as possible, aiming to have five points of explanation. Think about the purpose of this: does it fulfil its purpose? What is the rationale behind it? Finish your response with an example in order to gain full marks. The biggest problem in similar questions on the current specification would be candidates writing responses that are too brief and failing to offer enough detailed explanation.

**Question 3** (15 marks) – A longer question requiring more detailed explanation of a range of points, with the aim of giving one relevant example for each point in order to access full marks. Answer this question by clearly identifying, in a brief introduction, the range of points you will go on to consider. Then address each point clearly in a paragraph, with as full an explanation as possible, adding in an example for each paragraph/point, and at the end of the paragraph referring back to the original question to show how this point is relevant. Remember to refer to the source, where appropriate, and to be as detailed as possible. The marks will be awarded based on the quality of explanation and range of points. However, it is better to have three or four well-explained and evidenced points than to have seven points that have no explanation.

All of these questions will be based on a stimulus source, which will be at the start of the paper. The final question will be selected from a choice of two essay style questions.

**Question 4a) or 4b)** (25 marks) – a traditional essay question which will require you to make an assessment of a proposition or aspect of the topic. This answer will require balance in the response; relevant and well-deployed examples; a range of points on both sides of the argument; and a clear and detailed conclusion. Answer this question by writing a clear and brief introduction that demonstrates how you are going to approach the question and which gives an overview of the points you will be examining on both sides of the argument. **Do not** answer the question in your introduction – the proper place for this is in the conclusion. Start by outlining the arguments in favour of the proposition in the question, and carefully, paragraph by paragraph, address all of these arguments, explaining how they do this and giving examples as appropriate. Then turn to the other side of the argument. It is very important to do this, as it makes sure you have a balanced argument. You are expected to challenge the proposition in order to arrive at a balanced judgement. As with the first half of your response, put all of your relevant points into succinct paragraphs, with as full an explanation as possible and an example. One example for each point is more than enough, as too many examples may drown out your argument or result in a smaller range of points, which would weaken your essay. After carefully considering both sides of the argument, write a final concluding paragraph in which you answer the question directly.

In addition, there are some common mistakes which should be avoided:

1. In the first three questions, which have a stimulus source, you need to avoid overly relying on the source or, equally, not mentioning the source at all – both of these approaches will result in lower marks being awarded.
2. Neglecting to provide examples or evidence to back up the points you make will make it very difficult for you to support your argument and will result in a lower mark
3. In the longer essay-style question, failing to provide a two-sided or balanced response will result in a lower mark. Part of formal academic writing is learning to take into account different viewpoints on academic debates, and being able to incorporate these into your argument.

4.  Using too many examples at the expense of more points can lead to a lack of analysis. It is desirable to have a piece of evidence or example for each point being made. However, providing more than one example for each point can lead to an unbalanced response with more examples than points. This leads to responses that have a narrow range of points. Despite having lots of evidence, these responses will be limited and will therefore fail to result in the highest possible marks. The ideal situation is to have one point per paragraph and one example per point.

5.  Analysis is required in the extended essay style questions so try to avoid narrative responses that don't address the question. By referring back to the question at the end of each paragraph and making it clear how the information in that paragraph relates directly to the question, you can make sure you are developing an argument as you go along.

6.  Leaving out a concluding paragraph will prevent you from reaching the higher level. All academic essays should have a final paragraph, no matter how brief, which addresses the question directly. This will make a difference in your overall score.

# Resources

This is a list of suggested resources, which will add to your knowledge and understanding of the topics you will cover.

## Websites
www.ccea.org.uk – this should be your number one resource as it gives you all of the past papers, the chief examiners' reports and the specification, so you can plan your study, revision and hone your exam skills. The AS Student Companion for Unit 1 and the EEP document, which provides an exemplification of a top response, would be particularly useful.

www.executiveoffice-ni.gov.uk – this is specifically on the Executive Office (previously called OFMdFM) and will tell you what the Executive Committee is currently working on.

www.niassembly.gov.uk – this contains everything you need on the Assembly. However, do not expect criticisms!

www.nidirect.gov.uk – this is good for policies and information on general points of interest.

*Political blogs*
www.devolutionmatters.wordpress.com – this is a good quality political blog by academic Alan Trench.

www.huffingtonpost.co.uk – this does not regularly cover NI politics, but has some valuable articles occasionally, or when there is a big story.

www.sluggerotoole.com – this is an excellent political blog.

*Political party websites*
- Alliance Party: www.allianceparty.org
- DUP: www.mydup.com
- Green Party: www.greenpartyni.org
- People Before Profit: www.pbp.ie
- SDLP: www.sdlp.ie
- Sinn Féin: www.sinnfein.ie
- TUV: www.tuv.org.uk
- UUP: www.uup.org

## Current affairs programmes
*Spotlight* (BBC NI) is an excellent round up of main events.

*The View* (BBC NI) is good for an overview of main issues.

# Recommended Reading

Birrell, Derek, *Comparing Devolved Governance* (Palgrave Macmillan, 2012)

Birrell, Derek, and Cathy Gormley-Heenan, *Multi-Level Governance and Northern Ireland* (Palgrave Macmillan, 2015)

Cochrane, Fearghal, *Northern Ireland: The Reluctant Peace* (Yale University Press, 2013)

Cox, Michael, Adrian Guelke and Fiona Stephen, *A Farewell to Arms? Beyond the Good Friday Agreement* (Manchester University Press, 2006)

English, Richard, *Armed Struggle: The History of the IRA* (Macmillan, 2003)

Enloe, Cynthia H., *Ethnic Conflict and Political Development* (Little, Brown and Company, 1973)

Galliher, John and Jerry DeGregory, *Violence in Northern Ireland: Understanding Protestant Perspectives* (Holmes and Meier Publisher, 1985)

Hargie, Owen and David Dickson, eds. *Researching The Troubles: Social Science Perspectives on the Northern Ireland Conflict* (Mainstream Publishing, 2004)

McEvoy, Joanne, *The Politics of Northern Ireland (Politics Study Guides)* (Edinburgh University Press, 2008)

McGarry, John, ed. *Northern Ireland and the Divided World: The Northern Ireland Conflict and the Good Friday Agreement in Comparative Perspective* (Oxford University Press, 2001)

McKittrick, David and David McVea, *Making Sense of the Troubles: A History of the Northern Ireland Conflict*, rev. ed. (Penguin, 2012)

McMahon, Margery, *Government and Politics of Northern Ireland*, 3rd ed. (Colourpoint Educational, 2008)

Mitchell, Paul and Rick Wilford, eds. *Politics in Northern Ireland* (Westview Press, 1999)

Purdie, Bob, *Politics in the Streets: The Origins of the Civil Rights Movement in Northern Ireland* (Blackstaff Press, 1990)

Ruane, Joseph and Jennifer Todd, *The Dynamics of Conflict in Northern Ireland: Peace, Conflict and Emancipation* (Cambridge University Press, 1996)

Tonge, Jonathan, *Northern Ireland: Conflict and Change*, (Routledge, 2001)

———, *Comparative Peace Processes* (Polity Press, 2014)

Wilford, Rick, *Aspects of the Belfast Agreement* (Oxford University Press, 2001)

Wilford, Rick and Robert Miller, eds. *Women, Ethnicity and Nationalism: The Politics of Divided Societies* (Routledge, 1998)

Wilford, Rick and Robin Wilson, *The Trouble with Northern Ireland: The Belfast Agreement and Democratic Governance* (New Island Books, 2006)

Whyte, John, *Interpreting Northern Ireland* (Clarendon Paperbacks, 1987)

# Copyright

The author and publisher gratefully acknowledge permission to include the following copyright images:

# Index

# Disclaimer

This book has been written to help students preparing for AS Unit 1 of the Government and Politics specification from CCEA. While Colourpoint Educational and the authors have taken every care in its production, we are not able to guarantee that the book is completely error-free. Additionally, while the book has been written to closely match the CCEA specification, it the responsibility of each candidate to satisfy themselves that they have fully met the requirements of the CCEA specification prior to sitting an exam set by that body. For this reason, and because specifications change with time, we strongly advise every candidate to avail of a qualified teacher and to check the contents of the most recent specification for themselves prior to the exam. Colourpoint Educational therefore cannot be held responsible for any errors or omissions in this book or any consequences thereof.